OAK HILL
VOICES FROM AN AMERICAN HAMLET

AN ORAL HISTORY

BY

Michael Hayes

6/07
Oak Hill, N.Y.

Best Regards,
Michael Hayes

Bloomington, IN Milton Keynes, UK
authorHOUSE®

AuthorHouse™
1663 Liberty Drive, Suite 200
Bloomington, IN 47403
www.authorhouse.com
Phone: 1-800-839-8640

AuthorHouse™ UK Ltd.
500 Avebury Boulevard
Central Milton Keynes, MK9 2BE
www.authorhouse.co.uk
Phone: 08001974150

First published by AuthorHouse 4/20/2007

ISBN: 978-1-4343-0245-8 (sc)

Printed in the United States of America
Bloomington, Indiana

This book is printed on acid-free paper.

Cover photo: Early scene of Main Street (Route 81),
                Oak Hill, looking west up Christian Hill

The Oak Hill Preservation Association 2007

To the People of Oak Hill

"We owe our present to the past and it should give
us a feeling of obligation for the future."

Jessie Van Vechten Vedder

Acknowledgements

Greene County Historian Raymond Beecher and the staff at the Vedder Memorial Library at the Bronck Museum were extremely cooperative and helpful in providing me with assistance in my research.

Charles Soderblom, Durham Town Clerk, and the staff at the Durham Town Hall were generous with their time and with helping me sort through the numerous documents on file in their office.

I would also like to recognize the many people who allowed me to come into their homes and record their memories of Oak Hill. These same people were magnanimous in their sharing of personal photographs, letters, diaries and other indispensable primary source material. I especially would like to thank Helen Hulbert and Ralph Hull for their continued support from the outset of this project.

Melissa Woisin, colleague and friend, assisted me in presenting the graphics in this book. I am exceedingly appreciative of this help.

The Oak Hill Preservation Association has backed this work and encouraged it since its inception. Thank you.

Dr. Ronna S. Feit devoted an enormous amount of her valuable time to proofreading my work, listening to my ideas and offering countless suggestions, for all of this, I am grateful. Without her many contributions this book would never have been possible.

Forward

By Raymond Beecher

The history of a rural community is reflected in the inhabitants' ways of earning a livelihood, their social interaction with relatives, friends and neighbors and the extent of their interest in religion and politics. Occasionally a farther off event will stand out in a myriad of "down the decades" of recollections of the older residents. The label "Local History" has been given these aspects of daily living. Michael Hayes of Oak Hill and Long Island, New York has successfully gathered together for readers' enjoyment much of the township of Durham's local history as it relates to the hamlet of Oak Hill, where he is a resident. In this research and writing he was encouraged by Dr. Ronna Feit. They live in the Oak Hill "Old Parsonage" which has had the benefit of their kind hands.

I well recall periodic trips to Oneonta during my college years, using Route 81 which leads one through Oak Hill. It was my frequent practice then to slow the car down to low gear in order to admire the chain link embellished porches and also one in the Greek revival style. Some were closed and shuttered and occasionally in a summer in those eras I would get out to Oak Hill for an auction sale as the closed-up house contents were dispersed. With the general stores closed, employment scarce and old families passing on, Oak Hill was then a dying village. Today is an entirely different story as newer residents are attracted to the natural and man-made beauty of the township through which flows the Catskill Creek, fed by several tributaries. Like-minded residents have now banded together with the goal of historic preservation utmost in their minds; this non-profit group is the Oak Hill Preservation Association.

It is a truism that individuals purchasing a historic property sooner or later begin to ferret out the lives of the former occupants. Author and historian Michael Hayes is no exception. Researching primary and secondary resources he has brought together a wealth of Oak Hill history. In this effort he has not neglected oral interviews, which can be time consuming for a part-time resident.

The hamlet of Oak Hill is well represented on the Greene County Historic Sites Register and a number of its nineteenth-century houses display the oval bronze plaque. The same may be said for listing on the State and National Register. The Greene County Historical Society's Annual Tour of Homes periodically benefits from Oak Hill's wealth of architecture.

Author Michael Hayes is to be commended for his 2007 book. He sets a splendid example to other historians to take up the challenge for their Greene County Communities. He joins a notable company of local historians who have preserved local history for oncoming generations.

Preface

"Oak Hill! Oak Hill! That place is a ghost town." That was the response received in 1989 when we excitedly told an elderly local man that we entered into a contract to buy a house in the nearby hamlet. The fact of the matter is he was, largely, correct.

At one time Oak Hill had been a thriving community. Every house was occupied and merchants did a brisk business. But that time had come and gone. We took a walk down Route 81, also known as Main Street, in the evening after the closing. The rose- colored glasses now removed, we could see just how astute the old timer's observation was. The large and imposing Independent Order of Odd Fellows (IOOF) Hall was closed. DeWitt's Hotel was closed and looked as if it were about to fall down and Ford's General Store was empty. The old barber shop, ice cream parlor, Hall and Burnett's (formerly Tripp's General Store), and a dozen other structures were either boarded up or out of business and had been for many years.

That night I stood in the yard and peered out through the darkness at our newly acquired and dilapidated barn, silhouetted against the black sky. As I was about to turn and walk in from the autumn chill a shooting star tumbled through the atmosphere just above the barn. Being fresh from Brooklyn, where the wonders of the night sky are normally obscured by city lights, this was a thrilling sight. I interpreted this astronomical exhibition as a good sign and thought, "What a wonderful place."

Neighbor Jim Carlin often recounted that when he crossed the small bridge in Oak Hill and first saw the house he was to purchase as a retirement home he thought he had entered Brigadoon, the mythical town where time stood still. Ken Dean saw his house for the first time on a foggy eve, his would-be home shrouded in a mist that parted like a curtain as he neared the aged building.

Other people's introduction to the hamlet was somewhat more spectacular. Sara Stickler, for instance, relates that, in 1991:

> I was working on the second floor of the hotel and suddenly I saw out of the window two horses pulling a carriage and running madly down the road, Route 81, and they got to the Oak Hill Kitchen and the wheel hit the pole and they all went down. A woman then came speeding by in her car and jumped out, captured and restrained the horses. Luckily they were unhurt. That was my first experience in Oak Hill. I thought, 'What kind of a place is this?'

On any given day one will never fail to see some unique things. On Helen Hulbert's porch, for instance, there stood a pair of large wooden polar bears wearing Yankee gear. Once Norman Hasselriis was spotted in front of his house, also on Main Street, operating a bubble-making machine that had previously been used to create effects in Hollywood movies. He sat by the road on an old wooden chair, relaxed and quiet throughout the beautiful spring day as he slowly filled the hamlet with bubbles. Occasionally, someone would stop and sit beside him for a while, watch the bubbles float by, point, smile or laugh, then move on.

Oak Hill is situated in New York State's Greene County in the Township of Durham. It is a hamlet, the rural version of a city neighborhood, with only vague boundaries but is, for the most part, considered to be contained within the area of a particular zip code. Oak Hill's is 12460. It is approximately 20 miles west of the Hudson River and 35 miles southwest of Albany. Nestled in the shadow of the Catskill Mountains at about 700 feet above sea level, the hamlet has always been thought of as a place apart.

One woman, in 1938, tuned in to Orson Welles' "War of the Worlds" broadcast in which he fooled many listeners into believing that the earth was being invaded by creatures from Mars. She left her home to head for Oak Hill, thinking it so out of the way that even Martians would not be able to find it. In addition, Carol Cooke, while growing up on an Oak Hill farm during the height of the Cold War, didn't fear a Russian attack because she was certain that the Russians would not waste their time annihilating peaceful and sleepy old Oak Hill.

Walking up and down Main Street even the mildly curious cannot help but wonder about those who lived in the old buildings, a number of which are architectural gems. How did the people live their daily lives? What had they hoped for and what had they valued?

I was standing with a friend on Oak Hill Road, formerly known as South Main Street, near the eastern end of the hamlet in front of the Internally Gratefull Café. A lost motorist pulled up and asked for directions. After we answered his question he began to drive away but paused for a moment and said, "What is this place, the town that time forgot? You guys don't know how lucky you are." I decided to find out just how lucky we were by asking the oldest residents what they remembered about Oak Hill in days long gone.

After having conducted a few interviews, I developed a deep interest not only in the hamlet's history but also the way in which the older folks expressed themselves. For instance, the word *creek* was pronounced *crick*. It was evident from the beginning of the interview process that the elder citizens of Oak Hill paid little mind to politically correct language. A person might be described by their physical disability, like "the blind organ player" at the church or the telephone office employee who was "the crippled girl." In addition, people of African-American descent were referred to as "Coloreds."

I learned a lot of things, including how to prevent a skunk from "stinkin'." I found talking to these seniors to be an eye-opening experience and decided to share with others what I learned, through this book. I talked to younger people and newer residents, too. I also examined hundreds of pieces of primary source material.

I decided that I would focus my energy on writing the history of Oak Hill within living memory. Before long, however, I realized that it was essential to present some information on the origins of the hamlet and life in 19th century Oak Hill for the sake of continuity and to help develop a greater appreciation of the community's heritage.

Finally, some of the information presented will take the reader out of the tiny upstate hamlet to places as far away and historically pivotal as Gettysburg and Okinawa. In the end the protagonists always wind up in Oak Hill making their unique contribution to its character and history.

Contents

A Brief Early History

Indians

Animals created small trails in the woods and Indians followed those trails, making them larger and larger and then longer and longer. The resulting paths helped to facilitate movement between tribes and to enhance trade and communication. One such trail began in what is today Catskill on the Hudson River and led westward to present day Oak Hill, close to what is now called Route 81. The Lenni Lenape Indians, part of the Algonquin tribe, were divided into various sub-tribes with the Katskill Indians and lived around Oak Hill. They paddled dugout canoes and fished in the Catskill Creek, the very same creek that one day would see foundries, mills, railroad tracks and homes lining its bank. By and large these Indians were peaceful people that would rather present gifts of wampum to a potential enemy than to have to fight with them. But their numbers began to diminish in the 17th century when exposure to European settlers infected them with deadly diseases.

The Iroquois, from further west, had not yet been devastated by the diseases and were able to gain control over weakened groups, including some of the surviving Lenni Lenape. Other Katskills moved westward and joined with different tribes, thereby effectively eradicating the Katskill Indian culture and their presence in the area in and around Oak Hill.

The Iroquois sided with the British during the Revolutionary War, hoping that the "Red Coats" would assist in driving out the settlers. They participated in several raids in the area including one in Durham Township in which settler Hendrick Plank was captured and taken away to Canada, where he died while being held hostage.

However, with the American victory the Indians had pretty much lost all hope of gaining sole proprietorship over any of their former territory and so they moved westward or to Canada where the British granted them land. For a while Indians became eerie spectral and pitiable figures on the landscape in Oak Hill and its environs. Every now and then someone would spot an Indian at a distance peering out from behind a tree and then quickly vanishing into the mist of the dark woods. Eventually they were seen no more.

Early Settlers

In about 1771 Lucas DeWitt came to settle in what would become Oak Hill. King George III had granted a patent on the land to a Scot in the British Army, a Lieutenant Colonel named Richard Maitland. DeWitt leased the land from Maitland and his heirs. Other early settlers included John Plank and Hendrick Plank. This, the earliest settlement in Durham Township, was at first called DeWittsburgh. These founders built rough shelters, probably of logs, along the Catskill Creek and then began to farm. In 1780, when Indians killed two members of the Stropes family of Round Top in nearby Cairo and burned their home, Oak Hill's pioneers thought it prudent to abandon the settlement. They returned after the Revolution, sans Hendrick Plank. Gradually, by acclamation, the name Oak Hill would replace the far less graceful DeWittsburgh.

Tanneries were founded in and around Oak Hill due to the abundance of hemlock trees, the bark of which was used in the tanning process. Harnessing the power of the Catskill Creek, the lifeblood of Oak Hill, and its tributaries, settlers quickly developed saw and grist mills and before long iron foundries began to spring up. Oak Hill's Cheritree Foundry reputedly became the first such site to make practical use of the malleable iron process. The iron industry boomed and Oak Hill, noisy and polluted, grew up around it.

Railroad

The news of a railroad starting at the Hudson River in Catskill and extending westward about 40 miles to Middleburgh with a stop in Oak Hill was greeted with unbridled enthusiasm. The plan was that ultimately the railroad would continue about another 30 miles to the town of Canajoharie and from there have access to the Erie Canal. Raw materials, such as pig iron, were being hauled to the foundries and mills by horse and wagon. Quick delivery of raw materials followed by the shipment of finished products back to the Hudson River or on to Middleburgh and then to vast markets in the west could bring about a greater explosion of commerce in Oak Hill. It also held a promise of further development of industry in the burgeoning hamlet.

By 1838 construction was under way and by April 1840 regular daily rail service was provided. The locomotive, named Mountaineer, chugged, clanked and puffed its way into the hamlet on tracks laid along the Catskill Creek. In order to get to the hamlet the train first had to cross three bridges specifically built for this purpose by the Canajoharie and Catskill Railroad Company. The bridges were of lattice construction and were built with thrift in mind.

On May 4, 1840 the locomotive steaming towards Oak Hill with freight and passenger cars in tow, began to cross the second of the three bridges at a spot near the hamlet called High Rock. The center piers had been weakened by the roaring creek and the bridge collapsed just as Mountaineer made it to the western bank. The chains that connected the locomotive to the first car snapped and three freight cars along with two passenger cars holding about 40 people plunged into the rushing creek. One passenger sustained serious injuries to his legs and a few others were injured but not as severely. An engineer, a local man by the name of Jehiel Tyler, was killed.

A new bridge was constructed in just one month and service was restored on June 5. The railroad continued its normal operation until May of 1842 when, because of its tarnished reputation, weak financial backing, and lack of public interest and support, it failed. The tracks were torn up and other uses were found for the remaining equipment.

The loss of the railroad marked the beginning of a slow and inevitable decline of Oak Hill as an industrial center in the region. Factories moved away to locations better suited for their demands. It would take until the end of the 19th century for virtually all manufacturing in Oak Hill to dry up and die, but it did.

Prominent Resident

Lyman Tremain is said to be Oak Hill's, and arguably Durham Township's, most prominent resident. His father Levi Tremain moved near Oak Hill in 1812 from Massachusetts and finally by the 1850's settled with his wife, Mindwell, next to Saint Paul's Episcopal Church Cemetery in the eastern end of the hamlet.

Mindwell gave birth to Lyman on June 14, 1819. Although his earliest education was local, he later studied in Kinderhook and became a lawyer by the age of 21. His career advanced quickly. Lyman became District Attorney at the age of 27 and County Judge at 28. In 1857 Tremain was elected New York State's Attorney General. His final political post was that of Congressman, a position to which he was elected in 1872. His greatest accomplishment was when he, along with attorney Wheeler Hazard Peckham, successfully prosecuted "Boss" Tweed, New York City's most notorious crooked politician.

Tragically, Tremain and his wife Helen (nee Cornwall) lost three sons. One, Frederick, was killed in the Civil War while serving as a Lieutenant Colonel at a battle at Hatcher's Run near Petersburg. The strain from the loss of these boys may have been responsible for the premature deterioration of Lyman's health. He died on November 30, 1878 while visiting New York City. He is buried in Albany Rural Cemetery in Menands. His parents are interred in Saint Paul's Cemetery next to their former home. The IOOF Hall in Oak Hill was named in Lyman's honor.

Civil War

A number of men from Oak Hill and its environs served in the military during the Civil War. The following two stories are representative of the experience of these veterans.

In May 1861 when the 52 year old Reverend Henry H. Bates entered the service in Glens Falls he was gushing with earnest patriotic fervor. He was "a faithful representative of the Republican Party" who firmly believed in the indivisibility of the Union and was considered by many to be an abolitionist. In May, as he and the Twenty Second New York Volunteers were about to march south to war, Bates stood in the middle of them all and gave an enthusiastically received, stirring, and lengthy oration praising the soldiers' resolve for the great cause of union.

By all reports, Bates served the men under his pastoral care extremely well. In addition, he saw more than his fair share of combat, suffered with sickness and on at least one occasion slipped out of the very hands of the enemy. He wrote to a friend that he in fact "was saved from being taken prisoner by a New Jersey girl who more like a sister than a stranger watched over me and nursed me in my illness."

Two years after his rousing oration in Glens Falls his service as Chaplain drew to a close. It was a disillusioned and sickly man who was then assigned to Oak Hill's Saint Paul's Church. Although his patriotic fervor and Republican credentials remained inviolate no one could now rightfully label him an abolitionist.

He had seen things in Virginia that caused him to believe that those enslaved were not truly desirous of emancipation nor did they have, in his estimation, a bad life being thought of and treated as property instead of free people. After interacting with a large number of contrabands (liberated slaves) who were brought into camp he became convinced that 90 percent of them, as he wrote, "wishes himself back on de ole plantation this day." In addition to believing that the number of reported whippings was exaggerated, he thought the slaves to be hypocrites. Bates had come to believe that the black man's plantation life was easy in comparison with the rough life he led as a soldier.

The few years he spent ministering in Oak Hill were those of a dying man. Bates would never recover from the ailments he picked up while in the service and eventually they brought about his early demise. In January 1868 he was laid to rest in Saint Paul's Church Cemetery. A large obelisk marks the site.

In sharp contrast to the well-established, middle-aged Bates was a 22 year old Oak Hill resident named Nathan Augustus who, without fanfare, joined the Army in August 1862. He became an infantryman in Co. K, 120th NY volunteers. In July 1863 Augustus found himself at Gettysburg and about to have a life-altering experience.

He had arrived on the battlefield in the early morning hours of the second day of the largest battle ever fought on the North American continent. Late in the afternoon the 120th stood with other units about a quarter mile from the infamous Peach Orchard. A battalion of 1,400 Mississippians advanced. At first the Southerners met with stiff resistance but before long their ferocious charge overwhelmed the federal forces and soldiers of the 120th dropped by the dozen. A .58 caliber bullet struck Augustus in the right leg four and a half inches above the ankle, blowing away three-quarters of his fibula bone.

Taken to a field hospital, he had every reason to believe that one of the understandably overwhelmed surgeons would take the less than 15 minutes required to amputate his leg. Dozens of limbs had already been cut away that day and were piled up like cordwood near the operating arena in a large and gruesome mound. Augustus found himself among the lucky few. The medical staff fought valiantly and with success to spare him the horror of amputation and before long he was sent to Jarvis Military Hospital in Baltimore, Maryland to recover from his wound.

Over two months later his leg had yet to heal completely and he became a limping and pained fixture at the hospital. He passed the hours building fires to heat the ward. With the passage of time Augustus was growing somewhat embittered, watching as hundreds of wounded soldiers came and went, and as he learned about the multitudes of men who purchased their way out of the service for $300.

With the memory of Gettysburg still fresh in his mind, he wrote to Oak Hill friend Eli Peck, "...you said that the Fair was the 29th and 30th. I suppose you are all going and I hope you will have a good time. Eli, I saw my Fair at Gettysburg and I tell you it was a sad and hard Fair and Eli I don't never want to see another such a Fair as that was and it will long be remembered by a great many..."

Homesick for Oak Hill, he deserted in November 1863 and returned to the comparatively peaceful hamlet, but before long he was captured by military authorities. He was taken into custody on Christmas Eve and was returned to service.

His leg healed to the point where he was able to carry out his military duties and he gamely marched off to action once again with the 120th. In May 1864 he fought at the Wilderness in Virginia and for a time was missing in action. Later, he participated in the long, and for Augustus, lonesome siege at Petersburg. In the end he had grown to like "soldgren", as he called it, and was proud of his service to his country. He was present at Appomattox Courthouse when at long last Lee surrendered to Grant. In 1865, he returned to Oak Hill, where he went to work at an iron foundry as a molder.

Nathan Augustus lived in Oak Hill until his accidental death, in 1882, when he was killed by falling timber. Augustus is buried in the Oak Hill Cemetery, his grave marked by a small stone that

commemorates his military experience. Ironically, after escaping death
on numerous occasions on far off battlefields, he was violently killed
in his beloved safe haven.

Agriculture

Farming was always an important occupation in and around Oak
Hill and as industry slowly declined, agriculture began to come to
the forefront and serve as the economic backbone of the community.
One man, P.S. Kenyon, who owned a farm on the southwestern end
of the hamlet, was typical of the hard workers of the area.

In 1875 Kenyon noted, in short phrases, the work, social obligations
and activities in which he engaged over the period of one year. A
partial listing follows:

Picked apples, made cider, went to picnic, worked on road,
drawed out manure, got in hay, helped J. Utter load some
stone, saw wood, Church, pick up mail, chores, clean stove
pipe, buy pigs, take crops to market, attend mother's funeral,
made two stools, fixed grape arbor, town meeting, put up fence,
visit with friends, ploughed, paid bills, collected debts, drawed
brush out of orchard, put cow in with bull, press straw, sow
oats, sow barley, sow corn, sow buckwheat, sow potatoes, sow
rye, husk corn, wash sheep, hoe garden, shear sheep,...

Dairy farms dotted the area and local merchants stocked their
shelves with items that the farmer required. It was the local farmer,
then, that kept the General Stores thriving and the smaller shops'
business at a brisk level.

Religion

From the hamlet's earliest days religion played a key role in the development of the character of the community. Organized churches served to provide a social center and a base for the strengthening of values warmly embraced by the citizenry, such as caring for one's neighbor. The church also presented the people with a greater sense of fellowship, civilization and purpose.

The first church established in Oak Hill was the Dutch Reformed Church. Services were held in Oak Hill as early as 1787. By the 1790's a wooden structure had been built on the far western end of the hamlet on Route 81. Although at first the church prospered it wasn't long before membership began to drop off. The new settlers of Oak Hill were largely of English extraction and mostly preferred the Quaker, Methodist or Episcopalian denomination. By the 1820's the local Dutch Reformed Church was in dire economic straits due to low membership. By the mid-1830's it was closed and the building was dismantled.

While the Dutch Reformed Church was in steady decline the Episcopal Church was, conversely, on the upswing. In 1809 the first efforts were made to build an Episcopal Church in Oak Hill. It took until 1834 (just as the Dutch Reformed Church met its demise) but Saint Paul's Church was finally constructed, complete with a steeple equipped with a bell. Soon an elegant wrought iron fence produced in one of Oak Hill's foundries enclosed the property. Saint Paul's continued to prosper throughout the century.

The Quakers had a presence in Oak Hill as early as 1812. They held their monthly Preparatory Meetings in private homes in the hamlet. The Quakers' history of abolitionist activism lends credence to the oral history that Oak Hill was a stop on the Underground Railroad. By the 1820's the Quakers were holding their meetings in nearby Coeymans and the Quaker influence in Oak Hill swiftly began to wane.

It was the United Methodist Church that would have the greatest and longest-lasting impact upon the Oak Hill community, instilling its values on generations of residents. In 1859 construction of a large church on Main Street was begun and by the 1880's the church was completed and the congregation was thriving. In 1868, The Board of Trustees purchased a house three buildings west of the Church (the same house in which Nathan Augustus had once lived) and maintained it as the Parsonage for over a century. In addition, they purchased for use as a Church Hall a house on a nearby tributary to the Catskill Creek. Weekly religious services, Sunday School, dinners, charitable fund raisers, socials and other events made the United Methodist Church an essential cog of the hamlet well into the 20th Century.

Development

In the late 19th and early 20th centuries Oak Hill witnessed what could only be described as a building boom. Industry was nearly dead but more than a few optimistic citizens and entrepreneurial merchants thought investment in the hamlet was a good bet. The Episcopal Church was expanded, a large IOOF Hall constructed, the Fords added another building to their general store, and the competitive Tripps replaced their quaint General Store with a grand edifice that dramatically increased its size.

People seemed to believe that no matter what happened Oak Hill would go on as an important commercial, if not industrial, center for the region. By the mid -1920's a strong economy and technological advances combined to facilitate electrification, a new bridge and a new State road. Oak Hill had gone from an industrial center to a charming hamlet.

A Walk

"...just another morning..."

I'm going out to clean the pasture spring:
I'll only stop to rake the leaves away
(And wait to watch the water clear, I may):
I sha'n't be gone long – You come too.

Robert Frost

Alfred Burnett, a tall and slender man, was in a contemplative mood. Just moments before he had paid his respects at the grave of his grandparents, Alfred and Mariah Tripp. The old part of the cemetery rests on a hillock overlooking the hamlet and it is shaded by oak trees. The Catskill Mountains were off in the distance sitting majestically beneath an azure blue sky. There before him was Mount Pisgah to the southwest, then heading southeastwardly Mount Hayden, Ginseng Mount, Mount Zoar and in the far distance Windham High Peak. It was one very beautiful spring morning and it was the early 1930's.

Now, as he began walking he paused, turned around and glanced once more at the mountains. It seemed to him almost as if they were looking back. Indeed, they had been silent witnesses to Oak Hill's founding, its rise as an industrial hotspot and now its incarnation as an agricultural community and a thriving hamlet.

He strode down the cemetery road, about 200 yards, to Route 81, passing under the iron Oak Hill Cemetery sign. On either side of him grew wild geraniums and as the spring and summer drew on other wild flowers would materialize throughout the hamlet: poppies, columbine, creeping thyme, pink roses, daisies, black-eyed Susans and many more. He crossed the road, turned, and walked eastward into the main stretch of the hamlet.

Alfred had worked well into the evening the night before and so was getting a late start on his day this morning. He was an intelligent man whose parents had vowed at the time of his birth in 1901 that he would study at Cornell. He did attend but after a while left the school because he wanted to paint...houses. Although he made his living through physical labor he was immaculate in his appearance and always exuded a professional air, as if he had just changed out of a business suit.

This particular morning he had two things to do. First, lend a book to his friend, Leo Ford. Oak Hill residents were well-read, with the literacy rate impressive at nearly 100 percent. Second, he would walk over to the Saybrook Inn, on the other end of the hamlet, to meet his partner Leslie Wade and give an estimate on a job there.

In addition to the two painters the hamlet boasted, among others, a barber, three electricians, three plumbers, a dentist, a clergyman, an undertaker, a doctor, a veterinarian, a mechanic, a half dozen merchants, two teachers, a photographer and two carpenters. Also, there was a secretary, a stenographer, a clerk, two chauffeurs, an antique dealer and a manager of a tea room. It was, by all measures, if not absolutely self-sufficient, then very close to it.

He continued down the road, this section known as Christian Hill.

On his right was the home of Byron and Hattie Hall. Byron was his father's partner at Hall and Burnett's General Store and Hattie was his mother's sister. Hattie and his mother were the younger sisters of Isaac Utter Tripp who had run the store, under his own name, for many years but handed it over to his brothers–in–law when he decided to retire.

Next door lived Dr. Herbert M. Simmons, M.D., then in his early 70's. He had cared for the people of the hamlet for years but at long last he was slowing down. Soon he'd have to be replaced by a younger, more energetic man.

On his left was Burnett's own home that he and his wife Elizabeth rented for $8 a month. Just then Elizabeth, happy as usual, walked out the front door to greet him and hand him the book that he planned to loan Leo, *Myths After Lincoln* by Lloyd Lewis.

Resuming his walk he passed the Methodist Parsonage, an old white house, built in 1815, with green shutters on the windows and wooden arches around the porch. He nodded to Clarisse, the young Parson's wife, who was sweeping the front steps while her small child Charles, Jr. played contentedly a few short feet away. Through the front window Burnett could see the figure of the Reverend Charles Garrett, sitting at his desk, deep in thought and writing this coming Sunday's sermon. He was one of dozens of Parsons and their families that would occupy this house during a period of just over 100 years.

"Good morning, Alfred" his mother, Carrie, shouted merrily to him from the front door of the general store. She, wearing her white apron, was already at work for hours. He could see, through the oversized front windows, his father Calvin, pacing around inside the dark store with a pencil and pad, saying something to his partner about inventory. Business had slowed lately and was, barely perceptibly, getting steadily slower. Most people were making their purchases at Ford's Store up the street but Hall and Burnett's was determined to continue to make a go of it.

Just then a loud groan emanated from an open window upstairs over the store. Dr. Byron J. Hunt, the dentist, was drilling away on the tooth of a young Oak Hill resident, Joyce Poultney. He stepped, a bit more briskly, in front of the home of Isaac and Addie Tripp and of Alfred's parents. It was the home where he was raised, a two story brick building constructed around 1832 in the Federal style.

Trees line either side of the road. In full flush at the height of summer the leaves meet over the middle and a shady canopy cooled off much of Main Street. Recently installed electric street lights were positioned every few houses.

He passed in front of the old blacksmith shop. Behind it stands the white Methodist Church with its columned bell tower. Just across the street a few old timers sit on the porch of Cheritree's Inn, deeply absorbed in an intense game of checkers and relishing the peace of the morning.

In the early 30's Oak Hill had a population of somewhere between 150 and 200 people. A little more than 100 lived in the main part of the hamlet and the rest were scattered around the outskirts. Most of the residents were Democrats but the Republicans were on the rise.

About 52 percent were female and with a few exceptions they stayed at home and did housework. On the average they spent over 30 hours a week on meal preparations alone. They spent at least seven hours each week on laundry. In addition, women typically maintained a vegetable garden to help minimize the cost of groceries. Their days and nights were filled with hard labor as they cleaned the house and cared for their families.

Main Street, Oak Hill was not a place for single people. About 50 percent of the population was married. Men took their vows at a mean age of 24 and women 23, although a couple of women were married as young as 15. Nearly 20 percent of the hamlet had lost their spouse. Another 20 percent was made up of children under 19. The children were split 50-50 by gender and averaged about seven years old. The remaining ten percent or so of the population was made up of about eight single men of whom three were over 60 years old and two women of whom one was in her early 40's. There was but one single woman, in her early 20's.

Continuing on his walk Alfred crossed the street and passed in front of the DeWitt house, the home of the descendants of Oak Hill's founders. Then he walked to the small bridge spanning the tributary that bisected the hamlet and led to the Catskill Creek just 100 yards away. Standing on the other side of the bridge were two very young men speaking animatedly with one very old man by the name of Page Hoagland, known to most as P.T. The young men were friends Carl Ratsch and Sheldon Ives. They were so engrossed in their conversation that they barely noticed Alfred as he walked by and said "Hello." Alfred could overhear Hoagland encouraging Carl, who produced a weekly column about Oak Hill.

Carl had recently created a humble newspaper, *The Acorn*. In it he reported on the daily life of the people of Oak Hill and its environs. He named one column *"The Kernel of the News from Oak Hill and Vicinity"* in which he reported some of the more mundane and sometimes mirthful daily happenings of the local residents.

Entries from various issues include:

Mr. and Mrs. Raymond Gifford were guests at a chicken dinner at the home of Mr. and Mrs. Arthur Millet.

Raymond Hunt is employed at Roy Kelsey's farm in Cooksburg.

The Ives family entertained the Tompkins family at a frankfurter roast Saturday evening.

It is rumored that Mr. and Mrs. Shanahan have rented rooms at the home of Leslie Wade.

Willet Lounsbury was on a fishing trip last Sunday.

Mr. and Mrs. Huron are visiting their parents, Capt. and Mrs. Huron.

While crossing the state road near Ford's building, Arthur Millet had the misfortune to be struck by an auto. Mr. Millet received cuts and bruises about his head and arm and was taken to Dr. Simmons. We hope for a speedy recovery.

The many friends of Mrs. Mae Kellam are glad to see her back from the hospital after a minor operation.

Mr. and Mrs. Hayward Rivenburg and Mr. and Mrs. Bruce Disbrow and son were pleasantly entertained at the Ives home Saturday evening.

Lawrence Dean has been sick for the past week.

Howard Poultney finished butchering early this week.

Mrs. Ernest Ford was in Greenville on business Monday.

Francis Birchett, Sheldon Ives and Carl Ratsch had a ride Sunday afternoon in Carl's Model "T". A bumpy time was had by all.

Sheldon Ives attended the card party at Greenville last Friday night.

Ford and Ford have new concrete steps up to the rear door of their store.

Leroy Brandow and Willet Lounsbury were fishing last week. Mr. Lounsbury pulled out a fine bass.

Catholic services are being held in the IOOF Hall during the summer months.

Dr. Simmons has returned from a recent trip in New Jersey.

On a fishing trip on the banks of the Hudson Eugene Kellam pulled out a fine eel.

The Wade brothers are putting on a roof at William Palmers' in Lambs Corners.

Raymond Hilzinger and Alfred Burnett gave blood transfusions to William Davis of Albany recently. According to latest reports Mr. Davis' condition is improving.

The many friends of William Goff were glad to know that he will be out soon after being in bed several months with a broken hip and arm.

T.L. Ford is having a well drilled.

Many of our local farmers have finished half of their haying.

Howard Poultney is adding to his milk-house equipment.

Willet Lounsbury of this village has a new Plymouth car.

We have been having fine sap weather.

Once across the bridge Alfred passed a small dead-end road that local people call Pigtail Alley due to its corkscrew shape. Then he looked to his left and waved to Willet Lounsbury who stood in his barber shop, a small cigar clenched between his teeth, as he gave a haircut to the constable, Fred Anthony. Willet waved back with a comb. Everyone liked Alfred Burnett.

Mae Kellam appeared from the door of her tea room. Two ruby-throated hummingbirds hovered above her head until she waved and said, cheerfully, "Good morning," and the birds zipped away. In addition to the hummingbirds many other species of birds could be seen around the hamlet including: gold finches, black-capped chickadees, kingfishers, Baltimore orioles, cardinals, red-tailed hawks, great horned owls, blue birds, green herons, downy woodpeckers, scarlet tanagers, cedar waxwings and brown-headed cowbirds.

Alfred strode on past Schoolhouse Hill Road and the little ice cream parlor owned by the Hulberts. The road curved to the right, past the Laraway house, built around 1840, with its four large, impressive columns and charming balcony enclosed by a low wrought iron fence. On his right, was the newly built home of Tracy Tompkins, Oak Hill's premier electrician. Every now and then a car would rumble by and the occupants would joyfully wave.

All of the houses in the hamlet were lived in and most, over 70 percent, were owned by its residents. The average value of a home was $3,500. Those who rented typically paid $11 a month. The average household was small, having but three people, yet only four percent lived alone as compared to eight percent nationally. The mean age of Oak Hill residents was 36 compared to a national average of 26.

The great majority of the residents in the hamlet were Caucasian. A few people, perhaps a dozen in all, of African-American descent lived around the hamlet and were mostly laborers who had drifted north in search of work as a result of the Depression.

From in front and to his right Alfred could hear the tentative chords of a piano lesson in progress. Olive Hodges, a precocious youngster, was taking lessons from Marie Pratt, a widow in her early 60's. Mrs. Pratt's older sister Emma sat on the porch and rocked contentedly in the morning sunshine. Shortly, he past Potter's Funeral Home and noted Stanley Potter inside busily arranging flowers and chairs in preparation for a wake, a relatively rare occurrence inasmuch as most people held wakes in their own homes.

At last he arrived at Ford's store. Looking out the front window Leo watched as Alfred neared. Leo stepped out the door. "I was hoping you'd bring that." he said while reaching out to take the book. Leo's Uncle Ernest could be seen in the back right of the large store by the Post Office talking with regular customer and friend, Brooks Atkinson, a renowned theater critic for the *New York Times* who owned a home a few short miles away in Durham.

Just then, William Cobb slid between Leo and Alfred and entered the store, a long list of goods in his hand. He nodded to Alfred who nodded back. There was something about Cobb that Alfred didn't like but couldn't quite put his finger on. Leo said, "I'm kind of busy now. I'll catch up with you later." He retreated into the store. Leo stood next to Cobb who handed him the list.

On the side of Ford's Store a flight of stairs led to John Huyck's place of business, insurance and real estate. He caught a glimpse of Huyck as he disappeared into his office. Continuing eastward Alfred walked in front of DeWitt's Hotel, the Creamery, Elmer Felton's property, then the IOOF Hall and P.T. Hoagland's little novelty store across the street. Saint Paul's Episcopal Church was in front of him. To his right was South Main Street, and to the left Route 81 continued. He walked left alongside the Church and then past the cemetery with the obelisk erected in honor of Henry Bates. Set back from the road is the old Tremain family house. Then Harold Woodruff's store, called The Glen Royal, but popularly known as Woodie's. Next there was Woodie's home, then a patch of land that Charlie Newman used for farming, and then the Oak Hill Garage run by Hyatt Field.

Floyd Ives, father of Sheldon, suddenly appeared leading a cow across Route 81. "Have ya seen Sheldon?" "Yes, down by the bridge talking to P.T. and Carl." "Thanks." And with a wave he was off.

Next, Alfred approached the home of the Hodges family. Out front Roy Hunt and Ned Hodges were engaged in a friendly conversation. Ned rented the house from Roy, who lived next door. He walked past the Hunt place and before him lay a long stretch of flat ground. Farmland. Then, farmer John Hull, father of 14 and known as Pa John, accompanied by his teenage son Ralph rode by on a wagon pulled by two horses and shouted a joyous, "Hello there."

Three deer appeared on the distant side of a field of hay, at the edge of the woods near the creek, about 100 yards away. There are many deer around Oak Hill and other animals have made the hamlet home: raccoons, squirrels, chipmunks, woodchucks, rabbits, skunks, opossum, foxes, and the occasional coyote. And down the way the road curved and meandered in front of the old Tavern which had been moved just a few years before from across the road. Next was the Saybrook Inn also on the left. Inside, Leslie Wade waited patiently for his partner to arrive and to give an estimate on a paint job. It was just another morning in Oak Hill.

Entertainment

"What Not"

Often on a Saturday night the Oak Hill residents and those from surrounding areas would go out to dance. Frequently a square dance was held at the IOOF Hall and on occasion the road would be blocked off and there would even be dancing in the street. It was not uncommon to have dances in people's homes, too. Folks would gather in the parlor, the host having rolled up the rug, someone would play the fiddle and someone else the piano. A caller would shout out instructions to the dancers.

The IOOF Hall was a great place for card parties. The occasional movie or play was also an attraction and every once in a while the fire company would use the hall to perform a minstrel show.

Willet Lounsbury's barber shop was a central point for socializing. Often farmers would gather as early as two o'clock in the afternoon and play cards or shoot pool. Local man Floyd Ives, Jr., known as Junior, remembers that farmers like his father would play cards and "have the hired hand out there do work."

The shop was always thickly clouded with cigar smoke. One of the five Lounsbury children or their friends was constantly in and out. When it was World Series time or when Joe Louis had a big fight the place would be mobbed with Oak Hill citizens listening to the radio. Even though over 70 percent of the hamlet's homes had a radio, Lounsbury's barber shop was *the* place to be.

A more mundane activity, used to entertain the smaller children, would center on a slide show in the home. A sheet was hung to serve as a screen and a primitive projector, called the Magic Lamp, made of tin and lit by kerosene, would be utilized to flash pictures of simple scenes.

An interesting local custom was one referred to as a "horning." When couples were just married or sometimes just about to get married the neighbors would gather together and wait until the two had gone to sleep. Then they would strike, descending upon their home and firing shotguns into the air, ringing bells, "hooting and hollering" and blowing horns. The newlyweds would have to invite the group in and serve them coffee, cookies, cake or whatever else they had around.

Eugene Kellam remembered that his wife, who was not from the area, had been frightened by the experience. "The very next night she heard a noise and she got up and she said, 'They're coming back.' I said, 'Who's coming back?' and she said 'Your friends who gave us the horning last night.' I looked out and saw a big pair of white horses on the lawn, they got out and they were on the lawn. I guess it was a good sign because we had a good marriage until she passed away. We didn't make the 50th but it was a good marriage."

Everyone was drawn to Woodie's Glen Royal, especially the children. Woodie, as owner Harold C. Woodruff was known, had created an ice cream confection called the What Not which had chocolate syrup and marshmallow syrup and chocolate and vanilla ice cream with everything on it. To this day people who enjoyed this treat as children roll their eyes and smile simply at the thought of it.

Many residents were active in Oak Hill's Masonic Lodge, the Mason's women's group, known as The Eastern Star, and the churches. The Methodist Church often sponsored dinners and other social gatherings at their hall at the foot of Pigtail Alley.

School

"...you did your reading and you did your spelling..."

The schoolhouse was a grey building that consisted of one large room. The boys entered on one side and the girls on the other. There was a clothes closet on either side. The classroom was divided by a curtain down the middle. In the early 30's two people dominated the small building up Schoolhouse Hill Road: Mary Dingman and Elvira Bullivant.

Former students uniformly use the word "love" when describing their feelings for Mrs. Dingman. Mrs. Bullivant was generally remembered less affectionately. Donald Lounsbury recalled:

When I went to school in Oak Hill my brother and I got an awful beatin'. The teacher had a rubber hose. We had a colored family lived up above Oak Hill. The first day they were there we were wrestling or something and the teacher caught us there. The colored kid said we was just playing and she took my brother and me and she beat the hell out of us with that hose because she thought we was fighting because they was colored and we was white. They were good kids, everybody liked them. She had an awful temper, Mrs. Bullivant did.

Anna Hamm, Mrs. Bullivant's daughter, said that her mother once took a misbehaving boy by the ear and marched him down Schoolhouse Hill Road to his home to report him to his mother. However, not everyone had trouble with her. Eugene Kellam said, "Elvira was a redhead and she was a spitfire. But I got along well with her. I used to sneak up there and she'd take me in," remembered Kellam, "I was 3 years old, too young, but she let me stay."

Mrs. Bullivant was assigned to the younger children and Mrs. Dingman to the older ones. The students grew used to listening to the lessons on the other side of the curtain and the brighter ones would learn from both teachers in the same day.

"One room schoolhouse up Schoolhouse Hill Road, that's where we went to school," recalls Junior Ives, "We didn't have no kindergarten. It was nice, it was good. We had a big pot bellied stove and we had the wood to put in the stove and heat where you did your reading and you did your spelling. I don't know how many grades they went. Mrs. Bullivant was the teacher. Later, we went to a newfangled school, Durham School."

In the freezing cold winter months mothers would send their children off to school with a hot baked potato to keep their hands warm and later the children would eat the potato for lunch.

The Great Depression

"... we had it better than city folk."

The Great Depression had a devastating impact upon much of the United States. Although Oak Hill was not completely excluded from the dire effects of the severe economic downturn that held America in its grip for over a decade many survived the era with minimal stress. Most people in the hamlet didn't have much to start with.

The general feeling among the local residents was that they were poor but they never thought of themselves as underprivileged. Local life-long farmer Ralph Hull remembers, "We always had enough to wear and enough to eat." The self-sufficient nature of the community saw to that. Hull said, "Back during the Depression years you read in the paper that people stood in line for two hours for a bowl of soup. In fact, that's what made me go to farming. I said, 'Boy, if I had a little barn and a little land I wouldn't have to stand in line for no soup.' We lived all winter out of last summer's garden. I always felt that we had it better than city folk."

Everyone that could do a little something to help out did. Just about all the men went fishing and hunting for game to eat. Most families had a cow and a few chickens. Young Eugene Kellam delivered newspapers.

I delivered the *Knickerbocker Press*. I had 18 customers in Oak Hill but even at three cents a copy a lot of people couldn't afford it. I made 18 cents a day and I thought I was rich. I had a bike and the man who ran the garage was awful good to kids, Hyatt Field. He welded it together and he never charged me. I remember bread lines in Albany. I said to my mother, 'Why are all those people standing and waiting?' People were hungry there back then and there wasn't no work for most.

The hamlet was not without its share of hardship. Donald Lounsbury remembers that Oak Hill neighbor Lloyd Paddock used to tell him, "We had beans for breakfast, beans for lunch and beans for dinner." Lounsbury also can vividly recall the Depression era Christmas when each child received but one small present. His was a metal car, which he still has and cherishes.

Harriet Rasmussen, who spent much of her youth visiting in Oak Hill with her beloved Aunt Elizabeth and Uncle Alfred Burnett observed that:

Oak Hill was a quaint little town where many of the homes were still using outhouses. Some people were still bringing pails of water up from the well and putting it on the stove to heat for household use. People didn't look upon this as odd or a hardship. Even some of the families thought to be more well off didn't have running water. The first time that Elizabeth and Alfred had running water and a bathroom was in 1939 when they built their new house.

I think people in Oak Hill were a frugal lot. Many were from farms where they could raise much of what they ate. And so, they were not impacted so much in the area of being able to feed their families, unlike those in the city. Farmers were not used to having much actual cash change hands. Their wealth was in their land, livestock, produce, etcetera. Stores like Hall and Burnett's sold groceries, kerosene and general merchandise but most of the people had a running bill because they could not pay. So store owners would have felt the hardship of having to keep stocked up and not getting paid on time.

In fact, Leo and Ernest Ford had generously extended credit to local people for goods adding up to many thousands of dollars, much of which was never repaid.

Crime

"Well, I am going to try you out."

When asked if there was any crime in Oak Hill one long-time resident, Burt Mattice, responded, "Crime, what's that? We didn't even know what the hell crime was. Anybody do anything wrong they get the shit kicked out of them. No, we didn't have no problem up here at all. To my knowledge."

Junior Ives had to scratch his head and think hard to come up with a crime worth mentioning that occurred in Oak Hill during his many years here. "I can't remember much crime ever happening in Oak Hill. Once, though, I remember my brother Sheldon had a pair of shoes down in the garage and a pair of shoes was worth something back then. Somebody came along to distract him and at the end of the day he saw his shoes were gone."

However, a few old-time residents vaguely remembered that when they were children something terrible had happened on the eastern end of the hamlet. The year was 1935. Early on Monday morning September 9 Eugene Kellam rode his bicycle down Route 81 to deliver his newspapers. He passed Hyatt Field's garage and saw something that had never been seen in Oak Hill before. Dozens of police, medical personnel and attorneys had gathered at the humble home of a poor laborer. A State Trooper said, "Halt, son." "What happened?" asked a wide-eyed Kellam. The stony-faced trooper responded with just one word, "Murder."

In 1926, seven year old Olive Bell Hodges had started dancing for small change on the dusty roads of Clover, Virginia where her father Ned worked. Olive loved to entertain. Her father, who was about 40, recognized that she had talent and taught her to play the accordion. Ned was a slight man at 5'6"and 140 pounds but he was a hard worker. He was a farm hand, laborer and he repaired roads. Her mother Carrie, 27, had her hands full raising a fast-growing family.

When the Great Depression hit, the Hodges family drifted northward in search of work and finally settled in Oak Hill in the spring of 1932. In addition to Olive there were her older brother Robert and younger siblings Dabner, Lee, Mollie, Lena, Carrie B. and Dorothy. The family moved into a small wood frame house on the south side of Route 81. Ned worked on the county roads and served local farmers as a day laborer.

In 1933 Carrie died suddenly when she was eight and a half months pregnant. Now a budding teenager Olie, as Olive was known, worked to help support the struggling family. She toiled as a waitress, hotel worker and a domestic. Somehow she found the time to learn to play the piano and the guitar.

The oldest child, Robert, moved a short distance away and was working at the Glen Royal Hotel in Durham. All the other children had enrolled in school and had a number of friends in the hamlet. Life was a struggle for the Hodges family and, although Carrie's death caused them deep sorrow, by 1935 they were beginning to find hope in

Oak Hill. But then Olie became involved with William Cobb, setting into motion a chain of events that would lead to a tragic conclusion.

Cobb was born in 1900 in Sparta, Georgia. He had attended school for a grand total of five months and could neither read nor write. He was arrested a few times for petty crimes involving drunkenness and gambling. He was, however, a good laborer and in search of work he moved northward with his wife and four children. He went from job to job first in Schoharie County and then Greene County. Cobb and his family moved to Pennsylvania where his alcohol abuse and his wife's interest in another man led to his being deserted by his family.

Alone and penniless he drifted back to Greene County and found gainful employment as a laborer on the Oak Hill farm of Howard Poultney, just over Eagle Bridge not far from Saint Paul's Church.

Cobb earned $30 a month plus board and worked hard for it. He was 5'9", 160 pounds and at 35 appeared younger. It was just a short walk from Poultney's Flats, as Howard's farm was known, to the Hodges home where Cobb quickly became a friend of the family.

Cobb, also called Will, got along well with Ned. He thought Ned to be "a pretty good man." They visited back and forth quite a lot. Cobb ate dinner with the Hodges family often and from time to time Ned and Will went out drinking.

Things began to go wrong when one night in November 1934 following a few drinks and dinner Cobb and Olie were intimate. They continued to have sexual relations on a fairly regular basis for the next ten months.

Occasionally Cobb would even spend the night with Olie, slipping upstairs after Ned fell asleep. Cobb started giving her a few dollars a month. Then in September 1935, everything changed. Cobb had lately been having the sneaking suspicion that something was wrong. He began to become wary of Olie and decided to keep a close eye on her. That evening farmer Roy Hunt showed up and began to drink with Ned and Olie.

Cobb said that he was going to go home but instead stood outside the small house in the darkness, listening through an open window. He heard the three, Ned, Hunt and Olie decide to go to a nearby bar and then he watched, silently fuming, as they drove off. He remained in the yard waiting for their return. He stood there for hours until the trio pulled up. Olie and her farmer friend stepped out of the car while Ned remained in the back seat, fast asleep.

Then, to his horror, Cobb heard the footsteps of the two climbing the stairs to the second floor. He walked to the car and could see Ned asleep. Will hesitated for a few minutes before he walked into the house and saw a lit kerosene lamp on the kitchen table. Taking the lamp he began to tip toe up the stairs but the two heard him creeping up and suddenly there was a rustling of blankets and clothes and then the sound of hurried footsteps. Cobb burst into the room where Olie lay in bed. He turned and stared into the doorless closet. There stood Hunt, pants in hand and wearing a look of absolute terror on his face.

Cobb demanded that he step outside and receive a beating. Olie yelled, "Will, you get out and stay out!" The farmer refused to go outside but Cobb was adamant. Finally, Ned awakened and rushed in to intervene in the mad fracas. During the ensuing debate Hunt, having by now put on his pants, slipped out the front door and sped off home. Cobb could be heard shouting at Olie, "Ain't you ashame? Ain't you ashame?"

The next day after the children were off to school and Ned had gone to work Cobb showed up at the door and tried to talk to Olie.

She slipped out the back, ran west on Route 81 and into the safety of the heart of the hamlet.

On Sunday, September 8, Ned, apparently having forgiven Cobb, went to Catskill with him and drank almost all day and into the night, finally returning to Oak Hill around ten o'clock. When they got back to the house they went to bed. Cobb sometimes slept in the same bed as Ned. Ned fell asleep but Cobb was not at all sleepy.

Olie had gone out that night to dance and drink at the Saybrook Inn with a girlfriend and two boys. Around 10:30 p.m. their car pulled up in front of the house. The car door slammed and within seconds Olie walked in and went upstairs. Cobb followed close behind. He came into her room sat on the edge of her bed and began to plead with her for reconciliation. She managed to get downstairs to the kitchen where he caught up with her, grabbed her and produced a pistol. She shouted to her father, "Will is after me!"

Before Ned could get into the room Cobb bounded out the back door. But once again he stood silently in the darkness outside the house. He could hear Ned shout, "God damn it, I don't know what is betwixt you and Will." Olie cried, "Nothing, nothing." Then she fled upstairs. Ned lumbered back to his bedroom and began to pace the floor. "God damn, I am going to kill Will Cobb if it's the last thing I do." Cobb stared through the window. "Well", he thought, "I am going to try you out." Walking at a steady gait Cobb headed back to Poultney's Flats. Meanwhile, Ned sat on the side of the bed and lit a cigarette. After he finished smoking he lay down and went to sleep.

Cobb entered Poultney's garage and grabbed a box of cartridges lying on a window sill. He placed them in his pocket and walked to the cow stable where Poultney kept his shotgun. He took the gun and put two shells in it, and then started back and a few minutes later arrived at the Hodges house. There he could see that a lamp was burning in Ned's room. He looked through the window and observed Ned lying in bed flat on his back less than three feet from the window. He thought, "Well, I am going to do a good job." He pulled the safety off and leveled the gun. Cobb pulled the trigger and the weapon discharged with a huge explosion, shattering the glass. Blood ran out from the side of Ned's head and onto the pillow. Reflexively, his right hand moved towards the wound but stopped mid-way and remained as a claw, like a sparrow's talon. Cobb stood still and stared for a few minutes.

Finally, he broke the shotgun open and emptied the spent cartridge, reloaded, walked around to the front of the house and climbed in through a window. Ned lay moaning, just barely clinging to life. Cobb sat down on the living room chair, took off his shoes and removed his jacket. He tried to relax in the pleasant, relatively dark room. The night air was cooling as he leaned back, the shotgun across his knees, the smell of gun smoke still wafting up from the weapon. He thought for a moment about catching a train and going someplace far, far away.

He could hear the children upstairs sobbing and he decided to wait for them to quiet down so that he could find the nerve to go up and kill Olie and then, finally, himself. He stood up and walked into Ned's bedroom, glanced at the now dead man, his slim frame lying limp. He extinguished the lamp. Cobb had felt the need to kill Ned so that the defensive father wouldn't interfere when he killed Olie.

Upstairs, Olie's little brother, Dabner, heard Cobb's footsteps as he walked to Ned's room. Dabner seized the opportunity to sneak down the stairs and climb out the back window. He made his way to the neighbor's house and awakened Raymond Hunt, Roy's son, who then called the State Troopers.

Meanwhile, Cobb stepped out the front door, took a match from his pocket, then calmly lit his pipe and had a quiet smoke. It was now raining lightly. He went back inside and sat down. Soon, State Troopers Fred Knight and S.L. Bulson arrived, sending shockwaves down Cobb's spine. He jumped up and rushed into the basement to hide. The Troopers broke down the back door, spotted the shot gun leaning against the kitchen wall and with guns drawn peered down the basement steps and shouted, "Whoever is down there come up with your hands in the air." Cobb replied, "Coming, Chief," and, meekly, he complied. He was quickly handcuffed.

Olie now hurried downstairs and told Trooper Knight that Cobb had a handgun. Knight asked him where it was and when Cobb said that he didn't know the trooper removed his glove and slapped him hard across the face. Later, the troopers found the pistol in the yard where Cobb had accidentally dropped it earlier in the evening.

Soon the house was utterly swarming with people including the coroner, the District Attorney John C. Welch and Stanley Potter. Potter, accompanied by Dr. Kenneth Bott, Dr. Lyle B. Honeyford, and the coroner, Dr. Mahlon Atkinson, transported Ned's body to Potter's Funeral Parlor where an autopsy was performed.

When the police informed Howard Poultney of what happened he stood motionless, shocked, dumbfounded. He had thought Cobb a faithful and reliable farmhand who could not be capable of committing a murder. He went to the barn with the police and saw, to his sorrow, that the twelve gauge shotgun was indeed gone.

By morning Cobb had been taken to jail, interrogated, confessed and held without bail. All of the Hodges children except the 22 year old Robert were held in jail in Catskill because the county had no immediate place to put this large group of orphans. Olie was held against her will as a material witness on $5,000 bail. She spent the better part of six months behind bars. However, along with her siblings, she was permitted to attend her father's funeral.

It was a pitiful group of mourners that gathered at Potter's to bid farewell to their beloved father. They all stood weeping quietly as Rev. Stanley Smith, Pastor of the Baptist Church of nearby Preston Hollow, conducted the service. The body was then transported to Oak Hill Cemetery where Ned was interred.

Cobb lived in the shadow of the electric chair for months, began to stand trial and was finally relieved to be allowed to offer a plea of guilty of second degree murder and was sentenced to 20 years to life. As he left the courthouse he smiled and said, "I am still alive." He was sent to Clinton Prison and remained there until he was paroled in 1952. Soon thereafter he quietly slipped into oblivion.

The children, sans the confined Olie, were all loaded on the back of a flatbed truck by a relative from the South and were returned to live in Virginia with their Aunt. Olie, who turned 17 while in jail, received a check for $241.50 for the time she was held as a material witness. She was now determined to settle down, look after her brothers and sisters and see that they got ahead. She returned to Virginia.

No one heard from any of the Hodges family again, except for once. Some 20 years after their unceremonious departure from the hamlet there was a knock at the door of the Oak Hill home of Bud and Helen Hulbert. There stood a well dressed young man that Helen did not recognize. "Is Bud Hulbert here?" The man asked. "Yes, I'll go and get him." When Bud came to the door he quickly took the hand of the man and shook it happily. He had recognized the young man right away and remembered him as a boyhood classmate on Schoolhouse Hill Road. Both men were smiling broadly. Bud turned and said, "Look, Helen. Look. You remember Dabner Hodges."

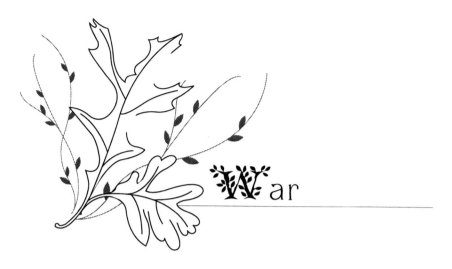

War

"Why? Oh! God, why?"

Starting with the Revolutionary War residents of Oak Hill served in every military conflict in the history of the United States. In fact, two young men of Oak Hill, John Dedek and Arnold Hull, were killed in Vietnam. The strongest representation, though, was in World War II when 28 men and women of Oak Hill were in uniform. All but one of them lived through their term of enlistment.

Army Private Earl Lounsbury, 19 years old, had one more night of leave to spend at home before he shipped out to England. That night, September 24, 1943, while driving with his date through Snyder's Corner in nearby Westerlo, his car crashed into a light pole and he was killed instantly. According to Eugene Kellam the girl, Helen Crop, survived the crash only to be killed in another auto accident years later.

Although Earl Lounsbury's death was a tragedy, Oak Hill was spared the loss of any more of its young men or women during World War II. While a number of Oak Hill's service members saw serious combat there was one who perhaps best exemplified the spirit of them all.

As a teenager he was known as "The Boy Editor of the Catskills." Carl Ratsch was to become one of the most popular residents of the hamlet. He dreamed of doing grand things in writing and publishing. The war, however, would dramatically alter those dreams for the rest of his life.

Carl, the son of German immigrants Otto and Helene, was born in nearby Cornwallville in 1913 and raised on the precipice of Oak Hill. By the time he was 12 he was already interested in printing and started his own business. His fascination with communication led to his writing a pamphlet for boys on how to make a telegraph set. Next, he went on to publish a monthly magazine for young writers that he called *Progress*.

Carl was ambitious. In an interview for a local newspaper he said, "I don't believe that there's a short cut out to success. You have to work, no, even fight along the way. Perhaps working for success is more fun than actually attaining it. If ambition, interest and hard work will win the goal, I've started..."

Eugene Kellam said, "I remember Carl way back in the Sunday School days when he was our teacher. We also had a little group that Carl organized called the Acorn Boys. He liked to name everything he did with an Acorn in it. We put on minstrel shows back then down at the IOOF Hall. He took us on some camping trips. He was a nice guy, a real nice guy." Helen Hulbert said of Carl, "He was wonderful, he was like a brother to me."

Aside from his brief observations on daily life in Oak Hill he expressed his thoughts on the beauty of the hamlet and its surroundings. He could write well on fairly sophisticated topics that reflected the values he learned in the hamlet's Methodist Church, as well as from family and neighbors. Later, some of these values would be challenged, when he was fighting for dear life.

In a column entitled *A Boy's Conception of Life* he wrote:

> Truly the world moves on faith. Without that great virtue all business and social activities would fail. Life itself would cease to mean anything. We sleep, secure in the faith that tomorrow will bring another sunrise. We eat, knowing that the food will give us nourishment and strength. We pray, with faith that our supplication will be answered and through faith in Him, life is made more livable... A young man starting out must guard well his reputation, so that people he comes in contact with will have faith in him.

He expressed his belief that there was an inexorable link between nature's beauty and God:

> Whoever has lived in the country has seen more of nature and been closer to the influences of its beauties and wonders. We see a crisp winter's evening, the ground covered with a blanket of snow; a deep blue sky above with a myriad of stars; a tall, silent pine silhouetted against the moon. Or it may be an early June evening, with warmth and fragrance in the air; the fresh smell of the soil, of new leafed trees, of lilacs and roses. A friendly spirit guides us as we walk alone. The sunset gone but a golden glow still lingers in the west. Perhaps a huge, full moon rises in all her glory and reflects on calm water at your feet. Nature is at her best...regardless of our creed or belief we find ourselves acknowledging a higher power, Nature-the Christian knows it as God.

As the years passed Carl became a pillar of the community. His circle of friends expanded as did his fledgling printing business. Then World War II broke out and he enlisted on March 25, 1942. He was 5'11" and, at 130 pounds, underweight with a delicate constitution and a few years on the average recruit. He made it his business to keep up with the best of them in basic training. His intelligence, hard work and affable manner helped Carl gain quick promotions and in practically no time at all he became a Staff Sergeant.

Before shipping out his unit went on parade and he described the event in a letter to his nephew back home:

Sonny! I was in a parade early last week for President Roosevelt. The President was only about ten feet from me when we marched past the reviewing stands. You cannot realize how great the precaution was taken to make sure the President would be safe. All men were searched, no outsiders were allowed. The place was covered with guns and secret service men.

The excitement of seeing the President would be nothing compared to the combat he was about to experience over the next three years in the Pacific.

First his outfit went to Hawaii where he was selected to study Aerial Photo Interpretation and Jungle Warfare. He then took part in a top secret briefing regarding plans to attack Guam. It wasn't long before he found himself making ready for a reconnaissance mission on a ship anchored off the coast of Guam.

He slipped overboard under the cover of darkness wading in water up to his armpits, across jagged coral, almost a half mile to the beach.

Soon he found himself close enough to the Japanese so that he heard them talking among themselves and he could smell their food and cigarettes. He observed some of their positions then stealthily returned to the ship, gave his report, and helped to coordinate the actions of the companies. The main force, armed with the information that Carl and others provided, climbed overboard and waded in for the attack, Carl with rifle in hand alongside them. For this and other acts of bravery the Army awarded him the Bronze Star.

The horror of combat, however, began to take its toll and it wasn't long before he began to question the values that he had heretofore held in such high esteem. "War is grim and horrible", he thought, "and hard for a Christian to comprehend in filth, gore and loss of feeling."

Between battles Carl would sometimes have to retreat to the comfort of the hospital to recover, for a few brief days, from the insanity of war. He often began to worry because on some occasions he was filled with enthusiasm and ambition and then again, "I sink into a rut of dejection, both physical and mental." He prayed that it was only a temporary aberration; otherwise it would be disastrous for post-war hopes and dreams.

When he returned to combat he found himself narrowly escaping death at the hands of Japanese snipers and mortar men. Soon, when there was a lull in the combat or when he was safely ensconced in a cave to escape enemy artillery, he began to crawl deep into a shell in his mind. For a brief while he was no longer on Guam or Okinawa but thousands and thousands of miles away in the Catskills...in Oak Hill.

He broke the year into six seasons of two months each and began, with shattered nerves, rotting feet and the constant chatter of machine gun fire and artillery bursts, to imagine he was home.

He thought, and later wrote:

January and February. There'll be snow, probably lots of it, and every body of water will be a miniature skating rink. There are many hills for the ski enthusiast and the folk with sleds and toboggans...every farm has a hill or two suitable for the amateur. The days will be cold and brisk, so bring along warm woolen sweaters, gloves and lots of warm socks. You'll have anti-freeze in your car and a set of chains for icy back roads. After a day in the cold, clear, bracing air you'll have a grand appetite that can only be satisfied by a good hot Catskill Mountain supper! The first few days you'll probably doze off early and want to head for a cozy bed, piled with quilts. After that you'll look forward to the beauty of a winter's evening: the blue lights of the moon on sparkling snow, a sleigh ride on an old farm sled, padded with sweet smelling hay or the jolly informality of an old-fashioned square dance. Maybe you'll like a game of cards by the fireside, with refreshments of cool apples and freshly popped corn with melted golden butter. Of course, you'll sample some cider, the champagne of the Catskills and...

Boom, boom, boom! "Jap artillery! Getting closer." He would abruptly snap out of his trancelike state.

The combat of Okinawa left him feeling "bitterly aghast at the seeming futility of it all." The first two weeks of May 1945 had been terrible on the front lines. Carl lived in caves and other holes in the ground. In frustration he'd suddenly start shouting, "Why? Oh! God, why?" Doubts would creep into his mind and he'd begin to feel that there was no God, but then, "knowing in the next sensible moment that there is and that He is very near and that He and He alone can help you out here on the brim of hell."

As the war entered into its final months civilians began to come out of the hills and caves seeking mercy.

He wrote home:

> This last trip I spent much time in a cave that was quite dry and a protection from enemy artillery and mortars. While up there some of the civilians were brought in, a middle-aged man, five small children and the shriveled old grandmother. They were found in a cave and were still blinking in the light. They'd been in the cave for several weeks, I suppose. They were pale, weak and dirty. They had sores on their bodies and flies all over them.
>
> One of the soldiers helped the old lady. The old man carried the baby piggy-back; a boy about six carried his two year-old sister. There was also a boy of about nine, quick, alert and seemingly strong and intelligent. They were a pathetic sight. For a ways I carried the five year old boy. He was quiet and listless, smelled like a corpse and had hundreds of persistent flies swarming over him. I could feel his small frail bones pressed against me through his thin jacket. Later I helped the old grandmother back through the mud to a jeep that was waiting to take her back to a civilian camp. She must have weighed 85 pounds and her old, wrinkled skin was stretched tightly over her old bones. She had the blue tattooing on the knuckles of her hands that is common to married Okinawa women. We gave them some food and water. I had the nine year old

boy help me wait on them by motions and the few Japanese phrases I know. These captured civilians are docile enough, always surprised at the good treatment we give them. Their soldiers tell them the Americans will torture and kill them. Some have committed suicide in thinking we would kill them.

Letters from Oak Hill boosted his morale. He heard from everyone, and he wrote back to all of them too: the Fords, the Lounsburys, the Hulberts, the Kellams, the Ives' and on and on. Even his famous friend Brooks Atkinson took time out to write to him:

I remember when you entered the Army - it seems to me about three years ago. For the last two years I was a War Correspondent in China and came home in November full of all kinds of Chinese diseases. You will be interested to know that we used up the last sheet of the writing paper you printed for us and are ready to give you another order just as soon as you knock the last Jap out of the Pacific.

Oak Hill was a lifeline to sanity and was at the root of Carl's faith. The bi-monthly descriptions that he conjured up in his imagination of the area in and around Oak Hill began to gel and he proceeded to write it all down. Soon he had the makings of a manuscript for a promotional pamphlet for the region that he would entitle *Return to the Catskills*.

Carl began to make plans for his own return. All he wanted was to build a home in Oak Hill and establish the Acorn Press. His dreams of great accomplishments were fading. He was happy to be alive and wanted just to be where, in his mind, he was always the safest during the worst of the war – Oak Hill.

When Carl got home he and Ernest Millet, his sister Helena's husband, built the Big Acorn Press just as Carl had imagined. Although he never fulfilled his youthful dreams of greatness, he did publish his heartfelt pamphlet *Return to the Catskills*. It was read by countless tourists throughout the region and went through two printings.

Based on his experiences in the Pacific he also wrote a draft for a novel entitled *Land of the Lavender Lizard* but it was never completed. He was a successful printer doing a lot of work for local boarding houses and for Stiefel, an Oak Hill based laboratory. He served as commander of the Durham Valley American Legion Post and President of the Catskill Valley Historical Society.

Carl spent the rest of his life in the house that he first dreamed up on a far away battlefield. The safety and peace that he prayed for was his and that, when all was said and done, was enough. He was diagnosed with cancer and it overcame him in early 1990. He was laid to rest in Oak Hill Cemetery.

"Some may find their best vacation pleasures by stretching out on the rich carpet of grass under a shady tree, closing their eyes and letting Nature take her course!"

From - *Return to the Catskills*

Sports
(Mostly Baseball)

"...a million dollar arm and a ten cent brain..."

Hunting was a favorite pastime of a number of Oak Hill residents, who generally hunted deer. In mid-November 1940, 16 year old cousins Eugene Kellam and Gordon Ahl drove Eugene's 1936 Chevy Coupe to Mount Pisgah in search of deer. The boys spotted a buck and fired. Then, suddenly, a gigantic black bear ran out of the brush in front of them and hastily lumbered away. Instinctively, the boys immediately fired and hit the bear twice but it kept running. Eugene chased after it, tripped on a low lying piece of barbed wire and as he fell the shotgun flew out of his hands and into the air in front of him. He thought the bear would be all over him but when he looked up he saw the animal seem to disappear in front of his eyes and then heard a loud "thump."

He picked up his shotgun and ran forward to a cliff and looking down saw the bear standing 18 feet below biting his shoulder in an effort to chew out a bullet. With Gordon at his side the boys began to fire down, missing a few times because of the odd angle and striking the bear a few times in the body, thick with several inches of fat in preparation for his impending hibernation. Finally, Eugene shouted to "shoot for the head." They fired and hit him in the neck and head and, at last, the bear fell dead.

The boys dragged the body a quarter mile down to the car. With help from a passing motorist they sat the huge beast up in the back seat and drove to Oak Hill, to the amazement of passing motorists. There were scars on one of the bear's paws indicating that he once fought his way out of a trap. They weighed the animal, hung it from a tree next to the barber shop, gutted it and measured it. It was over 500 pounds and was, from the tip of his toes to the tip of his nose, 9'2" long. According to Eugene, the newspapers reported that it was one of the larger bears in the Catskills. A bear feast was held at the IOOF Hall for the entire hamlet. Eugene said, "We were all inclined to love hunting and fishing and I guess we had it in our blood."

Fishing in the Catskill Creek was, indeed, a popular activity. Donald Lounsbury remembers trout 20" long being caught there. Skating on the frozen solid creek was a great way to burn energy. Donald also remembers leaving his house with his brothers on cold winter mornings, going down to the creek and skating from Oak Hill's bridge three miles away to Cooksburg, and back again, then repeating the trip all day long. In the summer some of the youngsters played softball. Swimming by High Rock and Dean's Mill near Eagle Bridge was also popular. But there was no question as to what was the most popular sport. Hands down, it was baseball.

Oak Hill had a good team in the 30's. Originally named the Plowboys, they soon became known simply as the Oak Hill Baseball Team. Although they could play well enough the team that really drew the crowds and attracted its share of excellent Oak Hill players was the neighboring Preston Hollow Sodbusters. "Most every town had a baseball team," said Eugene Kellam, "and Preston Hollow had the best one. They had a fella named Guy Dingman pitch for them. Guy Dingman was a good pitcher. He had long arms that reached halfway down to the batter. Oak Hill had its own team but the team that everybody knew around here was the Sodbusters." Donald Lounsbury remembered that Guy "had a tryout with the Yankees and the Yankees sent him home and they said, 'You got a million dollar arm and a ten cent brain, we can't use you.' But he was some pitcher."

Oak Hill's best players vied for a spot on the Sodbusters. They attracted huge crowds and many Oak Hill residents made the seven mile trip to Preston Hollow on Saturday afternoons to see the games.

They started out as a high school team called the Arapahoes and were formed in the early 20th century by Willard P. Elsbree who was senior partner in the Preston Hollow general store, W.P. Elsbree and Sons. After graduating, the team stayed together and eventually took the name the Sodbusters.

Bob Dingman and Pete Cooke, who would one day have neighboring farms on the south side of Route 81 in the western end of Oak Hill, made up the heart of the team. Roy Brandow of Oak Hill and a former catcher for a Durham team could be found at most games. "Roy Brandow was one of those persons that had means" remembers Willard Elsbree, descendant of the founder, "but I never knew what he did. He often was the umpire of games here. He seemed to like baseball and he often was there and they commandeered him to umpire." Alfred Burnett played for a while and then became a scorekeeper. Alfred Hulbert, who would become a member of the Oak Hill community, was an early member of the Preston Hollow team. The Sodbusters' first baseman was Donald Wade and his older brother Leslie played as well. Both were Oak Hill men.

The playing conditions weren't the best. The games were held on a rugged flat near the creek at the end of Preston Hollow. Hugh Elsbree, an early member and another descendant of the founder, wrote about the game in which Alfred Hulbert was about to settle under a lazy fly ball in a tie game in the 12th inning. He "stepped into a still wet cow-flop" and dropped the ball causing the Sodbusters to lose to Catskill four to three.

In his manuscript entitled *Twentieth Century Memories of Baseball in Preston Hollow* Hugh Elsbree wrote:

As an adolescent, Bob Dingman was a dashing, devil–may-care inconsistent player. Over the years he played many positions. As a shortstop for a few seasons after Delbert Wolfe, the original shortstop, left Preston Hollow, he was erratic, often half asleep. George Edwards (star Sodbuster) once grunted after Bob messed up on two or three grounders, 'You can't play ball after chasing girls all night.' After he married Mary Mitchell, then teaching in the Preston Hollow School, he settled down and he and George were, for many years, the backbone of the Arapahoes and the succeeding teams. He was a superb center fielder and after he had become almost crippled with arthritis, he was still a competent, steady second baseman.

A stranger watching him take batting practice would be bound to say he must be a terrible hitter. I have never seen a batter 'step in the bucket' as much as Bob did. A right-handed batter, his left foot would start going away from the plate when the pitcher started his windup, or motion if men were on base, and would go a full stride back. Yet he became a truly dangerous clutch hitter and could drive the ball almost as hard and far as George.

Elsbree also wrote of the time that Don Wade hadn't shown up and a game was scheduled to start. Elsbree asked Leslie and called over to Oak Hill but no one knew where Wade was. A few members of the team found him lying asleep, an empty bottle beside him. Elsbree wrote, "He had drunk a jug of hard cider and he was completely out." They got him to his feet and drove him to the game a few miles away in Medusa. "We pummeled him and yelled at him all the way. When we got there, he was bleary-eyed and confused." Still, he played an errorless game at first, hit two triples (that would have been homers if he were not drunk and unable to properly run the bases) and the Sodbusters won five to four.

The Sodbusters more often than not put on a good show for the fans. Their friendly rivals were the Middleburgh baseball team. On Independence Day in 1936 the Sodbusters swept no less than a triple header from Middleburgh. *The Middleburgh News* humbly reported that:

> July 4th may have been a glorious day throughout the country, but not for the Middleburgh baseball team. To lose two games in one day is bad enough but to drop three to the same team in the same day is the heighth of something or other. That's what the locals did Saturday. They lost three games to our friendly enemies, the Preston Hollow Sod Busters, and we take back all the cracks of the Sod Busters being old men.

The morning game was the only one worth watching, going eleven innings and ending in the score of three to two. Young

Bill Foland was Middleburgh's choice to cop the morning tilt and he was opposed by Pete Cooke. Both boys pitched great ball and both deserved to win, but in baseball someone has to lose and Foland was the unlucky one.

Johnny Zivelli was holding the Middleburgh sluggers to but three hits and no runs. Did you ask for the score? It hurts, but here it is, 18 to 0. In the third game the score was 16 to 7.

On at least a couple of occasions each year the Sodbusters played teams from the Negro League. *The Middleburgh News* reported:

Sod Busters to Play Black Sox - The Sod Busters, although widely known, must take a back seat for this famous colored team who have been bowling over semi-pro aggregations with the greatest of ease likened unto the man on the flying trapeze. The Black Sox, advertised as the greatest aggregation of colored ball players in the East, are a fast stepping group of men who take baseball seriously and have never been known to put up a poor exhibition of baseball. Comedy goes hand in hand with the most serious minded colored man and the game at Preston Hollow next Monday afternoon will not only be an exhibition of professional baseball as played by those who 'know how to play' but will produce original comedy as only the colored man can produce it. The admission price is .35 cents.

Most memorable, perhaps, were the games against the Negro League team the Brooklyn Royal Giants. In an earlier era the Giants were one of the most successful baseball teams in the Negro Leagues.

By the 30's the quality of the team had declined but they could still be a formidable foe. There was no question as to their entertainment value. When they played the Sodbusters they attracted crowds from far and wide and did not let down the fans. The games were remembered as always being exciting and, as often as not, the Sodbusters won.

The Sodbusters also played the House of David. A religious community, the Israelite House of David was established in 1903 in Benton Harbor, Michigan, by Benjamin Purnell and his wife Mary. Purnell encouraged the playing of sports, especially baseball, within the community. By 1920 the team began barnstorming the country to earn money for the community and to promote their religious beliefs. The team was always an attraction due to their long hair and beards, a doctrine of their religion. They started to hire players of quality who were not of the faith in order to stir up the large crowds.

As the years rolled by and the Sodbusters began to age, Hugh Elsbree wrote, "Baseball in Preston Hollow wasn't even a pale shadow of what it once was." Pete Cooke recognized the void and so thanks in no small measure to the efforts and devotion of this man by the 1950's Oak Hill had clearly become the baseball team to beat in the region.

In addition to the joy that the players experienced from being part of a successful team the families also shared in this great pleasure. The team and their loved ones were like a big family. On Sunday afternoons during the spring and summer months and well into the fall it was, for many, off to the baseball game. A picnic atmosphere prevailed. Cookies, hot dogs and sodas were sold at the games. Paid umpires called balls and strikes.

For a while they played in a field up Schoolhouse Hill Road but later played on land owned by Roy Brandow near the creek and Eagle Bridge across from Howard Poultney's farm. They had a lot of fans and scores of people would turn out to watch them play. Every town in the region had a team and they all took on Oak Hill with most falling short of victory. Going to a game of the Oak Hill Baseball Team was the thing to do.

Eugene Kellam said:

> Pete Cooke, I worked for him. The man could hit a ball harder than any man I've ever seen that was not professional. But he was a hardball player. He hit that thing so terrible hard when he hit it. As I said about three hits and he'd take the cover off that thing. He had awful powerful arms. He was a farmer and an awful nice man. I used to admire him.

Junior Ives recalled:

> Right where you call the Oak Hill Kitchen (IOOF Hall), they played basketball downstairs. Then, that one there, the DeWitt Hotel, we'd meet there for baseball when we started up in the spring. We'd see where we were going to play and who we'd play. We had a town league, see, we'd play Alcove, Ravena and Preston Hollow. They brought in the best players from all over. So the pitcher came and he would want to bring his own catcher.

By the late 50's and in particular into the early 60's the enthusiasm waned as Pete aged and more and more people began to stay home to watch baseball on television. In 1966 following the death of Roy Brandow his widow donated seven and a half acres to the town where the Oak Hill Baseball Team had played. The field, used to this day, was named in Brandow's memory.

United Methodist Church

"...a thorn in the flesh of the minister."

Arguably, the religious center that has had the biggest impact upon the greatest number of Oak Hill's citizens in the last 230 plus years of the hamlet's existence is the United Methodist Church (UMC). Construction of the simple yet elegant structure that would serve as the Methodist Church was begun in 1859 and when completed stood, with its columned bell tower, as a beacon for togetherness and love.

There has been, by design, a rapid turnover of ministers throughout the UMC's history, with exceptions such as Reverend Seaman and Reverend Arthur Magee, who stayed on through much of the 30's and 40's. But the driving force behind the UMC has always been its people and by the 1950's and 60's the church became the most important place through which one could hope to influence life in Oak Hill.

Meetings were held regularly at the Parsonage. There was a steady, solid backbone of church activists comprised of Oak Hill community members: Helen Hilzinger, Shirley Winnie, Junior Ives, Margaret Cooke, Leo Ford, Ruth Ford, Alfred Burnett, Loretta Lounsbury and a handful of others. The UMC owned the Parsonage, the church, a Church Hall on Giles Lane (formerly Pigtail Alley) and later another meeting place on Main Street called Smith Hall.

In addition to Sunday services, they organized fairs, picnics, Halloween parties for the youth, monthly suppers, guest lecturers, *Bible* study and presented such attractions as "Mr. Brand, a blind organist" who performed a recital at the church on a "new Hammond electric organ."

But not everyone got along all the time. In the early 60's Helen Hilzinger became involved in a bitter dispute with the pastor, Reverend Gordon Phillips, whom she had grown to despise. Miss Hilzinger wrote to the District Supervisor, "... please send our church a good minister...who can reunite the 90% of our people whose feelings have been hurt and rejected in our congregation by the unkind words and actions of our present minister ...Of the remaining 10%, one-half of those do not have a kind word for him."

At one meeting in the Parsonage the Pastor made "prolonged pleas to tell the people of his efforts to control his terrible temper and his weaknesses. The Minister was very angry that a Congregational meeting was called (in which his alleged shortcomings were enumerated) and he was not notified." The Minister's wife excitedly proclaimed that if anyone had anything to say they should, "Say it now or forever hold their peace."

Privately the Pastor and his wife thought of Miss Hilzinger as "a thorn in the flesh of the minister" and that the minutes, kept by Miss Hilzinger at the monthly meetings, "are loaded with personal animosity." But her supporters commented that he paid no taxes, no heat, and no rent, "Yet he is dissatisfied."

Reverend Phillips was also known for his kindness. For example, he helped following a tragedy when a local teenage girl killed herself. The girl's surviving two sisters, orphans, had no home. The Reverend and his wife took in the two, ages 12 and 16.

Eventually the Pastor was transferred. Resentment lingered and a Supervisor was sent by the Oak Hill congregation to the new home of the reassigned Reverend Phillips. The Supervisor had been asked to inspect the premises in search of furniture supposedly stolen from Oak Hill's Parsonage. None was found.

A later Minister, Dr. Edward Wren, noted in his report to his Supervisor that, "Oak Hill is ruled by a tight clique and they resent any intrusion on their domain." On the other hand Minister Orson D. Rice wrote, "We have in our parish good Methodists extending hospitality, friendliness, and good will and a concern for their Church."

Although the church often tried to help others locally they rarely acknowledged the tumult in the outside world. By the 1960's America was being torn in two by war, racial discord and a generational chasm but church meetings went on as if it were the earlier years, the 30's for example. However, on June 5, 1968 the outside world made a rare intrusion upon a church meeting when Margaret Cooke asked for a silent prayer for New York's Senator Robert F. Kennedy, who had been shot. (Margaret would go on to become Durham Township's first Councilwoman.)

By the late 1960's the influence of the UMC in Oak Hill began to wane. First they shut down the old Parsonage and transferred the Pastor to Durham, then put the building up for sale. Next, they tore down the old Church Hall. Leo Ford, a driving force in the congregation, suddenly died. Alfred Burnett also passed away unexpectedly on Christmas Day, 1970. He had come into possession of the blacksmith shop that was in front of the Church and he bequeathed it to the

UMC. They promptly tore it down. Eventually, services at the UMC were held only on alternate Sundays. Although the church remained active in Oak Hill its heyday was clearly now a thing of the past.

Decline

"...a band of young hoodlums."

By the end of the 1940's the decline began to show and no one could stop the slow and steady downward spiral of the once prosperous hamlet. As store owners died or retired the younger people were unwilling to stay on. Supermarkets simply made the old general stores unprofitable. The travel experienced by so many of the hamlet's young people during World War II coupled with the ready availability of quality automobiles and improved roads made it desirable and easy for the up and coming generation to leave Oak Hill and go far and wide seeking new opportunities. So, leave they did. The small dairy farms, once the economic mainstay, began to fail as larger faceless dairies took over the industry. It had once been a bustling regional center but now the hamlet had become a mere shell of its former self.

Stiefel Laboratories had flourished in Oak Hill and the residents benefited from its presence. In the 1940's Stiefel began manufacturing dermatological products in the old Creamery next to DeWitt's Hotel. They employed residents of Oak Hill and non-resident employees spent a healthy portion of their pay in the hamlet. By the mid-60's Stiefel was doing very well and was growing fast. The company needed more space and moved its operation out of the hamlet to nearby Route 145.

Early one morning in January 1967 a fire broke out in Stiefel's, then nearly empty. No one knows exactly how it started but a few people still at work in the building tried to battle the fire themselves. Chemicals stored there made it impossible for them to contain the blaze. The volunteer fire department was summoned at 4 a.m. but it was already much too late. The fire was out of control and burned well into the morning. The volunteers could only prevent the conflagration from spreading to the neighboring buildings, while the venerable old structure was reduced to a heap of smoldering ash.

One might trace the slow, at times almost imperceptible, but steady deterioration of Oak Hill from the train wreck at High Rock in 1840. The fire at Stiefel Laboratories marked the bottom of the downslide for the historic hamlet. With the possible exception of the building of a new firehouse it was, in short, an era of decline.

In addition to the Stiefel fire, Cheritree's Inn was razed. Lounsbury's Barber Shop, the ice cream parlor, Ford's Store, DeWitt's Hotel, the IOOF Hall, Hall and Burnett's Store, and more were all closed and still other structures were torn down or burned down.

In November 1978, Loretta Lounsbury appeared before the Town Board and expressed her concern for the elderly and shut-in people of Oak Hill. There was, she reported, a band of young hoodlums roaming the streets and threatening people. The elderly were afraid, she said. What Oak Hill had become would have been un-recognizable to the residents of the hamlet just a few short years before.

Throughout the 80's Oak Hill was largely just a sleepy old place with plywood nailed up over the windows of the once animated center of local commerce.

Rebirth

"Mom, I've done everything I've wanted to do."

In 1989, he stood transfixed and stared westward on Route 81. He was in front of the restaurant that he dreamed up a long time before. Sam's Oak Hill Kitchen. "You may think this is good but just wait. In five years this town will *really* be something." As far back as he could remember he wanted to achieve two goals. One, go to Broadway and help to produce great things through his work on the stage and two, open a restaurant.

Sam Stickler was born in 1955 in Kirkwood, Missouri. One time his father took him to visit a friend and the three went down to a basement coffee bar. As soon as he got home Sam disappeared into his own basement and when he reemerged, invited people down to see that he had created his very own coffee bar. He had strung up a curtain, served coffee and tea to a small audience and produced little shows. He was three years old. It wasn't that much later that he began to imagine opening a restaurant of his own.

Sam played records constantly. Years later his sister Sara would remember how he nearly drove her insane by playing and replaying the score from *Hello Dolly*, *The Music Man*, *South Pacific* and more.

Sara said, "You name it, he had it, and he played them over and over and over day and night."

Sam's father bought a house in a small town. "My brother and I spent the summer working on the house," remembered Sara, "he was supposed to paint the house but painted only the front because that is only what people, the audience, saw from the street." His parents didn't see it that way but it was Sara who got stuck painting the rest of the building.

As a teenager he wanted to leave home and go to New York but his parents wouldn't allow him to until he graduated from high school and then college and so he finished both in a total of six years, graduating with a degree in theatre from the University of Illinois. Then he was off to New York City's "Great White Way." He joined Actor's Equity and for a while he did lighting on the stage. When things slowed down in New York he went to California and worked for Max Baer, Jethro of television's *Beverly Hillbillies* fame. Sam worked as an assistant in the "B" movie business and was an extra in a few films, including the classic musical, *Grease*.

He returned to New York and began working as a production stage manager for different shows. His talent helped him to advance quickly and before he knew it he was meeting with great success. He was production manager for *Annie* and took the hit show *Evita* to South America. Before long he was working with Cameron Mackintosh, one of Broadway's greatest producers. He worked on *Oliver* and took *Les Miserables* to Europe. He also was the stage manager for Bernadette Peters' hit show *Song and Dance*. Taking these Broadway shows on the road was a logistical challenge that was nothing short of monumental.

Although everything was heading in the right direction in Sam's career, by the mid-1980's his world, the world of show business, was being hit unmercifully by AIDS. Friends were dying weekly. As Sam's friend, interior designer Thad Hayes said, "It was like a war." Sam began to look away from the city for an escape. He desperately wanted something that was decent and safe, a place where he could hide from the constant sorrow, pain, horror and fear. He wanted to create a kind of fantasy life where he could keep his sanity. Then the idea of the restaurant re-entered his consciousness. The whole notion of fresh home-style cooking touched a cord of comfort for which he yearned.

Thad Hayes owned a house on the edge of Oak Hill. While visiting, Sam was very impressed with the hamlet and it instantly captured his imagination. It appeared to him as a movie set all boarded up. He found it charming because it didn't have a lot of new buildings intruding on the classic architecture. Thad introduced him to his realtor and Sam bought a house on nearby Edwards Hill Road then set his sights on fulfilling his second dream.

Oak Hill appeared to have tremendous potential and he couldn't understand why people laughed when he spoke so highly of the place and the vision he held for it. He enjoyed the people of the hamlet. He convinced Cameron and two other friends to go in as partners with him, opening a restaurant in the old IOOF Hall.

The restaurant was an extension of his theater background. People asked who would come and, without hesitation, he answered, "Everyone will. Everyone!" He never thought of things as "you can't do it" but, rather, was an absolute optimist. He had a kitchen built on the stage, and put a window in front so that people could watch their food being prepared by the chefs. He combined his knowledge of the stage with his interest in food services.

The restaurant's grand opening in 1991 was the same day that the Greene County Historical Society held its historic homes tour in Oak

Hill. People did come, hundreds of them. Later, some drove as much as an hour and a half to eat at Sam's Oak Hill Kitchen.

Once the Oak Hill Kitchen was up and running he turned his sights on the old DeWitt's Hotel. He purchased the wreck and began to work on it right away to turn it into an antique store. Oak Hill was slowly becoming devoid of boards on the windows. He imagined the restaurant first, then antique stores would follow, bed and breakfasts would come after that. Sam had a vision for the hamlet as once again alive and a center of activity, neighborly camaraderie and commerce. The idea of resurrection appealed to someone who so recently lost many people close to him.

He stood looking westward on 81 thinking of all that the future held for Oak Hill when he realized that he needed to go to the doctor. There was definitely something wrong. His symptoms had been getting intense lately and were not going away. His check-up confirmed his worst fears. Now, he too was desperately ill and was dying, fast.

Sam could have returned to the city but instead wound down any pending business he had there. He could have gone back to Missouri or to his family's home in Florida but he chose to stay in Oak Hill because it had been the venue that helped him fulfill his dream. When he was on his deathbed among the last words that he spoke to his mother, Cora, were, "Mom, I've done everything I've wanted to do. I'm young but I did everything I wanted to do." He died soon afterwards. He was just 37 years old.

The restaurant was soon taken over by local chef Karl Dratz and re-opened as Karl's Oak Hill Kitchen. Sam's sister, Sara, now owns and operates the DeWitt Hotel Antiques. He did what he wanted to with his life but perhaps the greatest tragedy is that he never got to see how far he could have taken things. But Sam's efforts were a wake-up call for Oak Hill. As Sam's father, Lee, said, "He had really begun to rejuvenate the place."

As the 90's advanced people again began to buy homes in Oak Hill. One by one buildings that had been empty or neglected for years were being renovated or restored. Word had begun to get out that there were architectural treasures to be had in Oak Hill. In addition, as Sam once sought refuge from a horrible epidemic, following the tragic events of September 11, 2001 some sought refuge from terror in the remote hamlet.

Art

"...it's only simple when you learn to let loose."

Artists have always basked in an inexplicable magic that Oak Hill possesses. In the 19th century Olive Cheritree, of Oak Hill, was a young and gifted painter with a promising future whose career was tragically cut short by a severe case of mental illness. Eventually she died in a State institution but not before leaving an excellent representation of her talent in paintings that included images of Oak Hill. Hattie Tripp created impressive paintings of local scenes, P.T. Hoagland produced a wonderful series of Oak Hill postcards, Leslie Wade painted pictures and was a gifted photographer, as was local man Roscoe Delamater. In 1983 part of a feature length movie, *Hard Choices*, was filmed on Ives' farm. For five years beginning in 1989 David McDermott and Peter McGough, popular artists who create scenes of an anachronistic nature, made Oak Hill their home. Ralph Hull is a prolific painter to this day.

For 25 years the man who was considered Oak Hill's artist in residence was an unusual elderly gentleman who created sculptures from the strangest combination of items. He used everyday objects such as dolls (their heads mostly), springs, musical instruments, bicycle seats, children's sneakers, eyeglasses (sans glass), birdcages, paint brushes, goggles, footballs, stools, and a myriad of other odd things combined to create a form of art that was both whimsical and provocative. Norman Hasselriïs called his work his *assemblages*.

Norm was born on December 7, 1918 in Forest Hills, New York. His father, Malthe, was a well known miniature portrait painter and commercial artist during the 1920's and 30's. Malthe painted with such delicate precision that when observed through a magnifying glass one could see, in his portraits on ivory, distinct eyebrow hairs. Everything in Malthe's work was tight and realistic. Norm's mother Ruth was a homemaker but had taught piano until she had an accident and part of her hand was paralyzed.

Norm attended City College of New York for one year and having been deemed to be "4-F" by the selective service board during World War II sailed to Trinidad and worked as an assistant manager of a restaurant. Following the war he returned to the United States and took a job in advertising and publishing. He became a founder and general manager of Bantam Books' highly profitable Premium Ventures Division. Norm played the part of the successful businessman, wearing sharp suits and ties. (Many years later those same ties would be transformed into an impromptu assemblage.) But he never really liked any job he had. He did them simply to earn a living.

In the early 70's he gave up the business world forever to pursue his main interest, writing poetry. Norm said:

I had a pretty big job in the publishing business, and I saw myself self-destructing...and I began building an antique business, moonlighting. And through that I began more and more to play around with things I came across. In a sense, it was a re-education. I decided at one point just to drop out and gave up the job. I ran a little antique shop for eight years and decided that I was making too much money...so I sold out and moved...I came to the point where I realized I was corrupted by the power I had, running an independent corporation under the corporate umbrella. I did not have the capacity to carry the kind of load I was carrying.

Free from the corporate world he had the precious time needed to create poems. He did not yet think of himself as an artist. Then Norm opened a small antique shop in Queens, New York and began "playing around with objects and materials."

After four or five years Norm decided to sell the antique store because, "I had about six burglaries, four stick ups right in the middle of Richmond Hill." His first venture into the "country" was in Connecticut where he rented a place for a while and then began to look around for an adequate space to buy.

He had gone to summer camp as a boy in the upstate New York area and so the thought of returning to the scene of childhood freedom appealed to him. In his brief poem "A Tale of Two Cities" he wrote:

> born in
> simplicity
> moved
> to complexity
> going home (by way of eccentricity)

"And lo and behold," said Norm, "there was two nice buildings and three-quarters of an acre," in Oak Hill, "for $23,500 and that's when I moved in here with two truckloads of assorted junk and rarities." He had purchased what was once Potter's Funeral Home, built in 1840. Soon he began putting together the combination of items that would become his innovative, Dadaist sculptures. Norm gradually stopped thinking of himself as a poet and began to consider himself to be an artist.

He resembled someone Dr. Seuss would have dreamed up. Thin and bespectacled, with white hair and beard, he walked with a warped cane and was always dressed in a long-sleeved shirt, jacket and old hat even when the temperature reached 90 degrees and more.

The downstairs of his house was quickly filled with his work and transformed into a gallery. Norm's art spilled over into the garage next door. In the back of his house were a work bench and tools along with a 1,001 odd pieces of, well, junk. Every Sunday he could be spotted at the flea market in Preston Hollow with perhaps a bicycle seat under one arm and a dented Victorian birdcage in his hand. Soon these seemingly incompatible pieces of junk would be meshed together into a wondrous work of sculpture that would never fail to bring about a hearty laugh or even a smile to the face of the sourest of observers. In a way he was kidding the viewer and at the same time being a kid again himself. His work can be a paradoxical combination of amusement and something a little scary.

A pair of small stools with a painted duck head attached to each one. A bonnet on one and a sneaker and a propeller tail on the other. They are, of course, *Brother Duck and Sister Duck*. One work that he dubbed *"Impressions"* is comprised of a round piece of lumber with string for hair and bits of wood taken off of musical instruments creating a face that seems to have different expressions depending upon the time of day, the lighting and the mood of the viewer. *"Me"* is comprised of a large wooden box with a thick iron spring coming out of its top. A ball of yarn rests atop the spring and on the yarn are a tiara once worn by a first communion recipient and a pair of flip-up goggles protecting protruding lemon yellow eyeballs. When one moves the spring the image becomes laughably animated.

Norm had a funny way of naming his work. A potential client once looked at an assemblage, a small wooden bench with a bicycle seat for a head and a hinge for a tail and asked, "What do you call this creature?" After studying it for a long moment, with a small smile on his face, Norm responded, "I call it *Creature*." And then "What do you call this totem-pole like object?" Again a pause, then, "I call it *Totem-Pole*."

Much of his art was named with an air of descriptive simplicity: *Ukulele Man with Hat, Violin Lady with Beret, Two Sink Faucets Mounted on Pedestal Base, Gourd Man with Straw Hat, Box-Inside a Box Mounted on Thread Spool, Large Wooden Screw Dowel in Wood Block* and *Sawn Log With Buttons and Loop,* for example.

He saw his creative ability as play. "I just follow my childish impulse. I'm playing with my toys. That's the simplest way to put it. I don't see any limits. It's search and discovery and experimentation. It sounds awfully simple, but it's only simple when you learn to let loose." He had taken his art in the opposite direction of his exacting father in order, perhaps, to forge his own unique identity.

People just sort of stumbled onto Norm's gallery. Once Calvin Klein stopped in and admired a duck hunting jacket that Norm was wearing. Where the ammo was supposed to go Norm had placed harmless clothespins. He gave Klein the jacket.

For the last few years The Assemblage, as Norm named his gallery and workplace, was always open. Even when Norm left for the winter to go to Florida the door was left unlocked and anyone could walk in anytime and have a look around. Most of the time Norm was there and he would wander into his gallery and answer questions or teach a lesson on the meaning of his art to an interested young person.

In 2006, at 87 years old, Norm was dying. Just a few short months before he was happily going about his routine but suddenly everything changed. The doctors had found a tumor on his brain. When they showed him the x-ray he said, "Perhaps that lump is where my special creative ability comes from." They smiled and only wished he were right.

As his condition worsened he became completely exhausted and took to sitting in the back behind his gallery in a big old chair, covered in a blanket, completely dressed, including his camouflage hat. His Oak Hill friends and neighbors would shovel his walk, stop in to bring him food and help him take care of his daily business. On his work bench, usually filled with a myriad of odds and ends, there was now but one piece. A small ceramic doll's head, the skull cracked open, and into the void Norm had placed a red ball at just about the same spot where his own tumor was growing in his skull. This was his final work. As the winter wore on Norm moved to be with his daughter, Connie Eudy, and her family in Florida where he died.

People still walk to The Assemblage, then pause and stare in the window, nose practically pressed against the glass, a hand cupped on either side of the eyes blocking out the daylight. All of the work is there and it is all the same as he left it: timeless, incongruent, enticing, odd and, well, funny.

Religion
(Once Again)

"Why did Christians do little more than dress up...?"

*"Jesus said...'If you would be perfect, go, sell what you possess and give
to the poor and you will have treasure in heaven; and come follow me.'"*
(Matthew 19, 21).

The Twelve Tribes was founded by a group of people embracing
Christ's admonition to give up possessions. These were church-going
Christians in Chattanooga, Tennessee in the early 1970's. They listened
to the gospels and the sermons and they observed their friends and
neighbors who were content simply to attend church on Sunday and,
in their view, not fully embrace the teachings of Jesus Christ. This
small group wanted to be like the original disciples and they were
convinced that the Christian sects had gotten too far away from their
origins.

Then one Sunday it all came to a head. The church they were
attending cancelled their evening services because the Super Bowl
was going to be on TV. Even though the preacher had many good
things to say in his sermons, it didn't seem to make a difference, they
thought, in the lives of the people. They stopped going to church and

started being the church. They created their own movement and gave up their possessions.

Founded by Gene Spriggs and his wife Marsha, the members lived communally and respected, to the letter, the teachings of Jesus Christ (Yahshua, as Christ is known to the Twelve Tribes of Israel). The Twelve Tribes are theological reactionaries who are willing to give up the possessions which a great many Americans value so highly.

Spriggs wondered, "Why did Christians do little more than dress up in fancy clothes and meet in elaborate buildings...?" The *Bible* said to do "honest work with thine own hands to have something to share with those in need." They wanted to work together and share everything they had with each other. They opened the Yellow Deli restaurant to earn their living and have a place to discuss the teachings of Yahshua to anyone who wanted to listen. Their community grew quickly. The philosophy spread to France, Germany, Spain, Australia, England, Brazil, Canada, Argentina and across the United States.

In the late 90's the community purchased what was the DeWitt house and property. A small number of people, threatened by their presence, opposed them, and began spreading rumors in an effort to hurt the group. Among the most widely spread claims were that they would not pay taxes and that they would send their children to public school at local taxpayers' expense. Some people even said that Tribes members enslaved their own children and abused them. An open forum was held at Karl's Oak Hill Kitchen and people came from all around Oak Hill. The restaurant was packed and aspersions flew but The Tribes held their own and by the end of the evening had convinced enough of the fearful ones that they were not a threat and most of the trepidation was put to rest. After all, they did pay taxes, schooled their children at home and by all appearances were raising normal, healthy families.

In a spirit of cooperation, The Twelve Tribes wanted to participate in an Oak Hill homes tour sponsored, once again, by the Greene County Historical Society in 2001. One week before the scheduled event the headlines on the front page of *The New York Post* were dedicated to The Twelve Tribes. The paper suggested that The Twelve Tribes violated child labor laws. There was no hard evidence of any such behavior. They weathered the storm, participated in the homes tour anyway and greatly contributed to its success.

On most days members of the community will be seen strolling up and down Route 81, men with their beards and pony-tailed hair, women in their simple garb looking like 19th century aberrations, and plenty of beautiful, and well-behaved children.

In 2005 they purchased the IOOF Hall from Karl Dratz and opened a restaurant. At first things moved slowly. However, before long word got out and on some evenings, particularly in the summer, the restaurant is so busy that it's hard to get a seat. Some nights live music is performed and it harkens to a time when the old IOOF Hall was often filled with music and joy.

Oak Hill Preservation Association

"The hamlet is active..."

On a warm summer's morning in 2004 a small group of Oak Hill residents gathered around a table in the Internally Gratefull Café. With the sound of the Catskill Creek roaring in the background the conversation had focused on the recent controversy revolving around the home that was once occupied by the Tremain family. It had come close to being razed by the Town of Durham but in part through the efforts of some of the people at that table the house was saved.

Now the conversation shifted to the future of Oak Hill. They started kicking around different ideas about what could be done for the general betterment of the hamlet. They agreed that a not for profit organization could make a difference in helping to preserve historic Oak Hill.

Nick Nahas, who along with his wife Mary Lou, had purchased Hall and Burnett's General Store with its brick building in 1996, began to take care of all the bureaucratic requirements to start such an association. Then, later that summer, above the old store, a group of fourteen people gathered together for an organizational meeting of the Oak Hill Preservation Association (OHPA).

In part due to the Association's encouragement, ten Oak Hill structures on Route 81 were listed on the National Register of Historic Places. In addition, the Association has made every effort to facilitate the spread of knowledge and appreciation of Oak Hill. The OHPA sponsors guest speakers, publications, social activities, and public evevts.

On July 29 and 30, 2006 the first annual Oak Hill Days was held. In the parking lot where Stiefel Laboratories once stood the Twelve Tribes played music and danced in the steaming summer's heat, yard sales were held in front of Ford's Store, and throughout the hamlet. A pair of Civil War re-enactors held a small ceremony at the grave of Henry Bates and then traveled up to Oak Hill Cemetery to pay homage to Nathan Augustus. The gardens of several homes on Main Street were opened to the public. The hamlet is active and exciting once again. It has a long way to go but it has taken some tentative but giant steps towards forging a new identity that at the same time is linked to its impressive past.

Epilogue

"Waiting, for what happens next."

This morning, a fall day, the leaves are almost all down and blow around and around in the chilly air. One passes the building that was the Saybrook Inn where Alfred Burnett once painted and where Olie Hodges danced. Today, it is used as an upholstery shop. Next to it is the popular and busy Wayside Inn Restaurant. As the road curves, a stretch of farmland appears and up ahead on the right is a sign, "Oak Hill."

On the left is the old Hodges house all fixed up, painted, and a far cry from the rundown condition it was on that deadly night in the 30's. Across the road is the Ives place where Junior was born and lives today. Hyatt Field's garage is closed and has been empty for a few years. Behind it a small shabby trailer park sits. Woodie's former home is occupied but his old store is shut down for good.

The Tremain house is undergoing a dramatic renovation. The cemetery is well kept, as is the dignified and historically designated Saint Paul's Church, under Lutheran leadership since the 40's. The Twelve Tribes' Oak Hill Kitchen is open for business and a few community members are lounging around at the old Elmer Felton place next door. The parking lot has a few cars scattered around. DeWitt's Hotel is open for business as an antique store and its historical register plaque is proudly displayed in front with a thoughtful remembrance to Sam Stickler. The second floor of Ford's Store is an apartment and the ground floor is now being transformed into an art gallery. Ernest Ford's house is closed and rundown. Norm's Assemblage is locked. Mrs. Pratt's place has never looked better. The "column house" has a new roof and is freshly painted, making the structure look as wonderful as ever.

The house by the bridge where Helen Kellam grew up and that once served as a tea room and later a telephone office appears much as it always did. Up Schoolhouse Hill Road, the school has been renovated and is occupied as a home. The Lounsbury Barber Shop is closed. The houses on Giles Lane, once known as Pigtail Alley, are in excellent shape.

Just across the bridge the DeWitt house is filled with members of the Twelve Tribes. The Methodist Church sits, regally, but in need of a paint job. The brick house has been restored and Hall and Burnett's Store is open again as an antique store under its original name of IU Tripp. The Parsonage and its once-dilapidated barn have been restored and stand ready to welcome another couple of centuries. Alfred and Elizabeth Burnett's home is under renovation. Dr. Simmons' place looks much as it did that spring day in the early 30's when Alfred Burnett took his walk. Byron and Hattie Hall's home is now being renovated.

And just up Christian Hill the road to the Cemetery is the same and the sky is clear and blue over the old graveyard. Byron and Hattie Hall now rest there, along with Carl Ratsch, as well as many of the DeWitts. In an unmarked grave, Ned Hodges sleeps peacefully alongside Carrie. Helen Hilzinger, Isaac Tripp, Calvin and Carrie Burnett, Jim Carlin, Ernest and Bertie Ford, Leo Ford, Tracy Tompkins, Olive Cheritree, Nathan Augustus, Howard Poultney, Burt Mattice, Alfred Hulbert, P.T. Hoagland, August Stiefel, Hyatt Field, Sheldon Ives, Bob and Mary Dingman, Guy Dingman, Elizabeth and Alfred Burnett and so many more are all there. It is a very beautiful morning in Oak Hill and in the distance the Catskill Mountains sit majestically and, somehow, seem to be watching and waiting. Waiting, for what happens next.

Images of Oak Hill

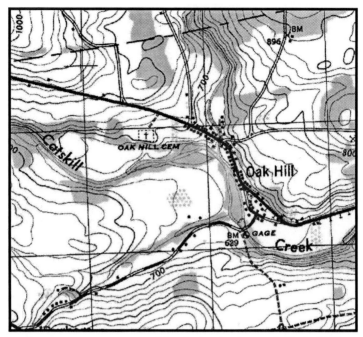

A recent topographical depiction of Oak Hill.

The western end of the hamlet.

The center of the hamlet.

The eastern end of the hamlet.

Scenic view of the Catskill Mountains
from western Oak Hill

Looking eastward on Route 81,
Oak Hill Cemetery road is on the right.
The late 19th Century.

During the 1860's, the home of manufacturer Walter Cheritree. Later it would serve as the Methodist Parsonage.

Addie Tripp, wife of Isaac Utter Tripp, in what would become Hall and Burnett's, c. 1905.

Calvin Burnett around the turn of the 20ᵗʰ Century.

The United Methodist Church of Oak Hill.

Hall and Burnett's and the Brick House.

Looking northward off the bridge, c. 1930.

Cheritree's Inn on Route 81.

The Upper Foundry

"...house by the bridge that once served as a tea room
and, later, a telephone office..."

Pratt's House.

Donald Lounsbury with a friend, Tony. c. 1956.

DeWitt's Hotel with Ford's Store to the west.

The Creamery, later Stiefel Laboratory,
in the early 20th Century.

The IOOF Hall named in honor of Lyman Tremain. Later,
Sam's, then Karl's and now the Twelve Tribes' Restaurant.

Saint Paul's Church.

The Icicle House down South Main Street,
today known as Oak Hill Road.

The swimming hole near Dean's Mill, 1920's.

High Rock.
Scene of the crash of the Oak Hill bound train.

An Oak Hill baseball player, Fred Hull, c. 1916.

Ralph Hull with nephew Gordon at
Meeting House Hill Road and Route 145, c. 1930.

The Acorn Boys preparing for a parade, 1932. From left:
Unknown, Llewellyn "Bud" Hulbert, Eugene Kellam, Earl
Lounsbury, Jack DeWitt and in the rear Carl Ratsch.

The Sunflower Girls, c. 1939. From left: Betty Lounsbury,
Phylis Barnes, Elenor Brockett, Dorothy Booth,
Helen Kellam, Betty Palis, Unknown, Shirley Burnett.

Mary Dingman in rear with her students, c. 1936. From
left 1st row: George Ford, Shirley Burnett, Lionel Ford,
Betty Lounsbury, Dick Wade, Eddie Vedder, Anna Paddock,
Evelyn "Tootsie" Smith, Junior Ives. 2nd row: Peter
Lounsbury, Tommy Woodruff, Norma Poultney, Harold
Smith, Violet Poultney, Viola Poultney, Jane Ives.

Donnie, Betty and
Peter Lounsbury in
front of the Hulbert's
Ice Cream Parlor, c.
1935.

Ernest Ford on his way to work, 1930's.

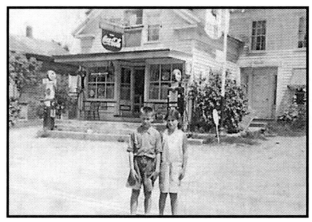

Peter and Betty Lounsbury in front of their father's
barber shop, c.1938.

The Ned Hodges murder scene. 1935.

The bear that Eugene Kellam and Gordon Ahl shot hangs next to Lounsbury's Barber Shop on Schoolhouse Hill Road, 1940.

In front of Ford's Store, early 1940's.

Vernon Magee, a Parson's son, in the backyard of the Parsonage, c. 1942.

Alfred Burnett, c. 1943.

Carl Ratsch, c. 1943.

Helen Hulbert (nee Kellam), c. 1944.

Earl Lounsbury, 1943, shortly before his untimely death.

A listing of the 28 Oak Hill men and women
who served their country in World War II.

The Preston Hollow Sodbusters. From front row left:
Clayton "Kick" Wood, Guy Dingman, Reg Makley,
George Edwards, Charlie Radick, Sr., Bob Dingman.
From back row left: Hayward Rivenburg, Dow Haskins,
Calvin Lacy, Hugh Elsbree, Pete Cooke, Jim Ronan.

The Oak Hill Baseball Team, c.1957. From front row left:
Ed Beechert, Bob Dingman, Ed Van Auken,
Clifton Richardson, Pete "Fred" Cooke, Lionel Ford.
From back row left: Herb Dratz, Charles Salisbury, Allan Winans,
Richie Connors, Herb Stiefel, Pete Woodruff, George Ford.

Sam Stickler outside his beloved restaurant, 1991.

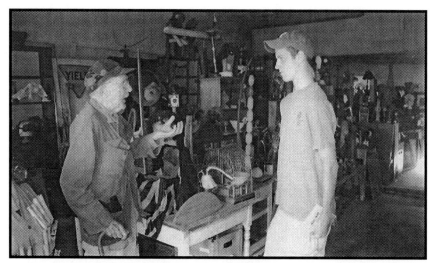

Norman Hasselriis explains the nuances of his art to young visitor Tom Burns at The Assemblage, 2005.

"Today life is a lot easier. Now I have so much spare time and I don't know what to do with it. When I could have used it I didn't have it." Helen Hulbert, 2005.

"I was born in '30 right in this house, upstairs."
Floyd Ives, Jr., 2004.

"You didn't need the goldarn TV to sit and watch all the while or a computer." Eugene Kellam, 2006.

"I think life was better in the old days. We had awful
good neighbors." Ralph Hull, 2005.

"Oak Hill had everything back then when you stop and think about it." The late Joyce Hull, 2005.

"Whenever I ride past the flat stretch by the Ives farm it takes me back to those days." Harriet Rasmussen, 2004.

"Money never changed hands we just helped each other and that's the way we operated." The late Burt Mattice, 2004.

"But I'll tell ya, when I grew up in the 30's it was like a big family, everybody helped everybody." Donald Lounsbury, 2006.

Appendix A
RECOLLECTIONS

Much of what appears in this book is the result of interviews with former and present residents of Oak Hill. In addition, I interviewed several people who lived near Oak Hill or had frequently visited the hamlet. What follows are excerpts from some of those interviews along with a brief introduction to each. Note that some people have a tendency to jump from topic to topic rather quickly.

Floyd Ives, Jr. lives on the farm where he was born and where he enjoys talking to his visitors, especially about the old days in Oak Hill.

My family came to Oak Hill for better land...soil. You go through Windham before you hit Ashland and there's a road, Campo Road, that's where they came from. The reason they were up there in Ashland, in the first place, was yellow fever. Somewhere in the middle there of the 1800's it came through the valley and they went up there. Dad was born in 1892 up on that hill. Up on the hill red shale growed potatoes real good. My brother, Sheldon, was born in 1915 and he went to school in Windham, pert near a mile downhill, on his hand sleigh. Better soil though is the reason they come here and got 100 acres. Now we have 200. The soil was a lot more deep out here right next to Catskill Creek. My family, they came in '29 from Ashland.

I was born in '30 right in this house, upstairs. There was no electricity here then. The guy who wired Oak Hill was Tracy Tompkins. He put the lighting in. This street light outside this house right here was the first one in Oak Hill. But he did put electric lights from up here through the village. Had to be in the early 30's.

I started working on this farm when I was six years old. We had a hen house out here and in the summertime or weekends mom would say, "Ten o'clock, go out and get them eggs." I had to grab the eggs and bring them back. We had good food. Better food you'll never see again. Beef, ham, tomatoes, beets, beans, whatever you want was down the cellar. Whatever you want it was all down the cellar.

Religion, back then everybody went to Church. There was Lutherans and Methodists. There was about eight of us with Sunday School and Ed Goff taught us. There was one guy who couldn't read too good and we'd help him, you know a younger guy, with the Scripture. Taking turns, each one would read a paragraph. When it was over we went to the crick and had hotdogs and hamburgers and we'd go swimming, boy what a time.

Then this store, that went down hill, right here in town, Woodruff's, where the Glen Royal was, that was a nice place.

118

It went down hill, it's too bad. That was a nice place...Woodie's. There was a pool table and we went there every night and we would play all night. You could play till 9:30 p.m. He would be open at seven o'clock in the morning and close at six o'clock and open again at seven o'clock 'til 9:30 p.m. and for 20 cents you could play. There was some that once they got beat they wouldn't come back for a while. My brother was one of the best around, he could really shoot pool. He was good at sports, pool, anything.

The Parsonage, I been in that building many years ago. In fact we went there for a horning. A horning, years ago when you got married they come 'bang-bang' and wake you up about one o'clock. Years ago that's what they did. They come with their horses and sleighs. Everybody would come and there would be a whole bunch they would come and get you out of bed, that was the deal.

Those days, I'd like 'em back, yeah, sure I would. Back then kids were protected too. I didn't go to a cemetery until I was 19 or 20. See, you didn't have all of what the kids have today; it's all there on TV. It's all told right there. Years ago you weren't told. You didn't have all that heartache.

Helen Hulbert lived in Oak Hill since 1927 and resided, until recently when she moved in with her son's family, just a few feet from the house where she spent much of her childhood. Typically, she can be found at the kitchen table poring over stories about the New York Yankees or talking about the history of her hamlet.

My mother and dad lived in Cheritree's Inn in the early 1920's when they were first married. Later they moved to the first little house on River Hill. It's still there near Saybrook Valley Road, where I was born in 1927. It was part of Oak Hill. My birth certificate says Oak Hill.

There was a little cider mill up there and my father worked at that cider mill. It was a rustic looking building, it's gone now, but you go up Saybrook Valley Road, used to be a big bar there but now it's a furniture upholstery place, across the road about a quarter mile and there was a cider mill on the crick.

My father was killed on a Sunday. I was one and a half when he died and my brother, Eugene, was five. Dad was home working on his car or something and had on a ragged jacket. Somebody asked him to go and do some cider and he did. He turned on the machine and his jacket got caught and there was no one there to shut it off. He got caught and pulled into the machine. He was young. His name was William Kellam.

After my father died we moved into the red house that is by the bridge on Route 81. My mother, Mae, had a tea room there and Dr. Simmons, who used to live nearby, ate there every day. He had a cocker spaniel and my mother would put out a plate for him and one for the dog.

Later, the house had the telephone office on one side. My mother was the operator there until 1943 or '44. Wilma Bates, Evelyn Alger, Rachel Stewart and the crippled girl, she had polio, Evelyn Clark, worked on the switchboard. My mother made $60 a month plus rent from the telephone company.

On the other side of the house were three brothers: Denny, Fred and Will Anthony. They were bachelors, never married. Will carved his initials on the well stone that's out here. There are stairs to the cellar in the house that are stone stairs. One night Denny came home drunk, he drank a lot, and he opened the wrong door. He fell down those stairs. He was dead at the bottom. My mother sent me down to get canned food in the morning and I was the first one to see him down there. I was nine or ten.

In the same cellar there is an indentation in the wall there that looks like a fireplace and they say they used to hide runaway slaves down there. It was always said that it was a stop on the Underground Railroad. I don't know how true it was. There are a lot of secret passages in the house. I loved it.

Just on the other side of the bridge Clark DeWitt had a huge iron foundry in the back by the crick. It was closed. We used to play on it when we were kids. We weren't supposed to be in it because it was dangerous. It must have been three stories. The caretaker was Mr. German and he had a whole bunch of kids and he lived in a little house right alongside the crick. It's gone now, too.

I used to walk to the store constantly. Hall and Burnett's across the road. As soon as mother got the money, then off I went to pay the bill for the last month. My father left no insurance and it was hard for her. Every commodity you needed was there. I remember a loaf of bread was nine or ten cents and the lady behind the counter told me "When you grow up it'll be $2," and I said, "No way!"

When I was four I used to go from the telephone company here and up the hill to the school house. Elvira Bullivant was my teacher and she didn't like me and she slapped me on the hand with a ruler. I told my mother that, "I quit!" but the next day I lined up with the others and went up Schoolhouse Hill Road. All the children were taught in the same room. Mrs. Bullivant taught the younger children and Mrs. Dingman taught the older ones. I loved Mrs. Dingman. Margaret Hunt, Mrs. Dingman's daughter, recently told me that she could take the eighth grade exam when she was little because she could hear what was being taught over the partition.

I remember coming down off Schoolhouse Hill Road on a sled and getting hit by a car. Mostly it hit the sled. I mean, I went flying through the air. My mother came out from the telephone office and she passed out. I thought the car had hit her. When I came to I said, "What happened to Mother?" and everyone said, "It's you, you caused it." You used to go from the top of the hill there all the way down to the garden. There wasn't much traffic, I just picked the wrong time. I wasn't hurt at all. I don't know who hit me. I have no idea.

Down the road at the IOOF Hall they used to do minstrel shows there, the local boys did. There were like ten young boys and they put on plays, showed movies. They were called the Acorn Boys and the leader was the one who ran Acorn Press, Carl Ratsch. We had the Sunflower Girls.

In around 1944 I went away to college and my mother moved into what had been the schoolhouse. I got married and moved into this house, right next to where I was raised, in 1952. I remember playing in the sand when I was two and watching them build this house for Tracy Tompkins. I was a practicing nurse for 45 years and raised six children here. Today life is a lot easier. Now I have so much spare time and I don't know what to do with it. When I could have used it I didn't have it.

Joyce Hull lived in Oak Hill for 75 years. She was the wife of farmer Ralph Hull. Joyce passed away shortly after completing my interviews with her.

I was born up in the Hollow in '23. When you go into Bates Hollow, don't turn for the church, go straight about a half mile beyond where the turn is and that's where I was born. Daddy moved us down here to Oak Hill in the spring of 1930 when I was seven. I lived on the first farm across the bridge from the icicle house, that's where I lived. My mother died when I was two and daddy married Marie and they had three more girls. So, they're all dead. I didn't expect to be living now. I mean, I'm the oldest one.

I used to walk over to school in Oak Hill. My twin sisters and I walked over. I used to pick up young Bud Richmond up on the corner at the icicle house and take him by the hand and take him up to school. I didn't have to but his mother wanted me to. The first year he went up pretty good but the second year he didn't want to. His mother was afraid that when he went up to 81, that he'd get hit.

My father, Howard Poultney, was one of three boys. His father wasn't much of a farmer. Fact is, my mother said that when her mother heard she was going to marry my father she didn't think much of it because she heard that his father milked his cows sitting in a rocking chair. My father became a dairy farmer and he'd have 40 cows, at the most. He kept Guernsey cattle. He was quite a prosperous farmer. He got up in the morning about five o'clock and he'd work to seven p.m., about.

I walked up 81 many, many times and I remember it like it was today. Where the trailer park is there was a house and a barn. A man and his sister lived in there and they kept a cow and a few chickens and in that field where the trailer park is they grew potatoes. My father put the trailer park there in the 50's.

But, many things have not changed. First, there's the Church, Saint Paul's. When I was a little girl they didn't have church there very often. I think once or twice in the summertime they'd have church there. Then that old hotel was there pretty much as it is now. Next, Ernest and Bertie Ford ran Ford's Store and they had the Post Office in there. Ernest, he was kind of the head man in Oak Hill, good man, kind man, he trusted people. Upstairs Jack Huyck had his insurance office and Ann Richmond was his secretary.

Marie Pratt lived a few buildings down and that's where I learned and took piano lessons. I think she was a widow or maybe she was an old maid. I never learned to play much because I was scared to death of her and she was a starchy old lady. Next, Tracy Tompkins and his wife Laura lived where Helen Hulbert lives today, and they had one daughter, Evelyn.

Way up 81 on the left is Oak Hill Cemetery. When I was a girl you didn't know anybody being buried there but they expanded it and started burying people there again, I think in the 50's. Nobody back then or hardly anybody was buried from the undertaker parlor. Back then, you call and he'd do you up and send you back home.

We got married in '40 and we came down and bought the farm in '44. Oak Hill had everything back then, when you stop and think about it. They sold gas in five places, Ford's Store, Hyatt Field's Garage, Lounsbury's Barber Shop, Woodie's and the fifth was Dean's Mill. You had the stores and the undertaker, a hotel, lawyer, doctor, dentist, and a veterinarian. Oak Hill was a quite prosperous place. It had about everything you wanted right in Oak Hill. I don't think that Oak Hill changed that much but it has. I think it's like when I was a little girl but it's different.

People come along now and they say Oak Hill is on the upgrade. But for a while there Oak Hill was pretty well run down. Back in the 20's and 30's it was quite prosperous. Things go up and down and get down low enough so that people could afford to buy them and fix them up again. I like the modern stuff. I liked my neighbors back then and I like them now. We had a pretty good life.

Ralph Hull lives today just a short walk from where he was born some eighty-eight years ago. On most days you can find him working on his art or garden. He contributes his wisdom and know-how to help advance the Oak Hill Preservation Association.

One of my grandfathers on my father's side was an original settler of the Town of Durham up there named John Hull. He came from Durham, Connecticut in the late 1700's. They settled up there on top of Meeting House Hill because they would have the advantage over the Indians. They would have the advantage of being on top and shooting down on the Indians. They had 17 different buildings up there. They had two churches, blacksmith shops and everything they needed up there to form a community, but it was so cold that they couldn't stay up there. It was so cold that in the first three years about a third of them died from pneumonia or the flu or something else there. They found out that the Indians were friendly so they moved down off the hill and into the valley.

In the Greene County history or something it told the story in there that John Hull was a small but strong man and very determined. He came home one time and a wolf was eating his sheep and he took the wolf and broke his leg over his knee and he let him go and the wolf never came back. He was a small man but he wasn't afraid of nothing. That was John Hull.

I was born in 1918 right at the end of WWI in Durham on 145 there. If you go up into Durham on 145 and turn left, it's the first place up where the big concrete wall is and the house up on top of it. We always had enough to eat and we always had warmth. We had 14 kids. We were poor but I think that the other kids were envious of us because we lived on a farm. We could have rabbits and we had little calves out in the barn and little pigs. We always had enough to eat and enough to wear. Except, once I ripped the pants out in the morning and when I came home at noon time I had to stay home until my mother could make new another pair.

One time my brother and I were just skipping stones out on the water by High Rock and I threw one and my brother said, "Why'd you throw it away?" and I said, "Well, it was a nice skipper." We were just skipping them out across the water, you know. Actually, it was an Indian sinker that went onto the lines for fish, to hold the line down. It was just so big and round with a hole in the middle of it. Now that I knew what it was I wish I never skipped it across. You know where the Durham Center Museum is, High Rock is about a half mile right behind it, and that's where I found it.

High Rock, that's where the train went over into the crick. Up there on the left beyond Oak Hill that was where the turn around was up above where the Twelve Tribes has their woodshop now. If you go up in there and look you can find the stones where the train would turn around. But on one of the first trips it went into the crick and never got there.

Dean's Mill was not far from High Rock. Silas Dean was the first one that I can remember in the 30's. He was probably in his 80's then. They sold rakes, plows, lumber. A gas tank was there too. They sold all kinds of horse supplies, harnesses, a ring to put in a bull's nose. You could get almost any farm supply you wanted in there. They sold feed and ground a lot of wheat and made flour and buckwheat flour. My dad would bring a couple of bags of wheat and it would be stone ground. They had two big six foot stones. When they ground buckwheat flour the shucks would kick out and the farmers would pick them up and use them for bedding for the cattle. No charge.

After Silas then Jerry run it and then Lawrence and he run it for quite a while and then his boys. There was a fire there a few years back. They're up on 145 now and Jerry Dean runs it. Dean's Mill was one of the more important places around, you know.

I remember there was a big Creamery next to the IOOF Hall. They made powdered milk there. I can remember when they made powered milk they had big rollers blowing steam and they made powered milk used for cattle feed and stuff like that. The guy who built that little house there, Elmer Felton, he run the Creamery. It was a butter factory and somewhere back in the 20's they brought cream in from up in the hills and all around and they shipped it to New York in little pound packages and some 30 and some 60 pound tubs. Stiefel took it over as a soap factory and it burned down probably there in the 60's.

Halloween night there was always all sorts of pranks. My brother, Fred, and his friends were in a Model T one year and outside Oak Hill they saw a wagon with a load of chicken manure on it. They got a hold of that and one man stood on the back end of the Model T Ford and they went along and saw a skunk and one fellow jumped out and grabbed the skunk by the tail. Of course, if you hold it by the tail they won't make their smell. So, he was on the running board with the skunk. They had been picking on these old folks and they had called the deputy sheriff and he opened the front door and the fellow on the running board, he let the skunk go and he flew right across that porch and into the front door and let his scent go and the other fellow in the back, he let go of the manure wagon and it flipped on the front lawn and that old Model T went 'putt-putt-putt' down the road.

Clark DeWitt was a veterinarian and he farmed a little bit. Behind his house was the old Cheritree Foundry. It was maybe 30' by 50' and was studs and boards. Probably closed in the 1800's, somewhere along in there. I heard my dad tell about it. In the winter time they'd take down beef and pork and butter and bring it down to boats in Catskill and bring back sugar and molasses and stuff. My father used to draw pig iron up from Catskill to the foundries in Oak Hill. The foundries were closed up by the time I was around.

Woodie's started to build in 1928 or sometime and he was gonna put in false window sills to hide alcohol. He had a little bit of everything. "You have to carry what everybody wants but can't find it anywhere else," he told me. The boys went at night and played pool. It was a gathering place for all the young folks.

I think that life was better in the old days. We had awful good neighbors. But today we hardly know our neighbors. If you had a pile of wood, you'd call your neighbor and they'd come and cut up 25 cords of wood. Maybe two or three nights a week we'd go and visit with one neighbor or another. I'd say we were very happy.

Today Lionel Ford lives in Florida but returns annually to visit in and around Oak Hill. This summer he took the time to discuss Oak Hill, in particular as it related to his family.

My great uncle was Ernest Ford, he was my grandfather's brother and he had the store for over 60 years, from the time that his father passed away. Ernest's father was Emerson. Emerson's father probably started the store in the mid 19th century. Emerson passed away suddenly when he was going to the store from a basketball game. The original store was torn down in approximately 1965 and was next to the building that stands today, and that was built in the late 19th century.

My father was Leo Ford, a lawyer in Florida, and he was right across the hall from my grandfather's law office. He was in business for about a year when the Depression hit, in 1926. The Depression hit in Florida first. He had lots of business but nobody could pay him. He decided to go to work with my great uncle. My great uncle had everything that you could imagine back then. The store opened about six o'clock and closed about 9 p.m., six days a week. The store closed at about two in the afternoon on Sundays and Christmas was at four.

They had hardware, paint, clothing items and at least a thousand rolls of wallpaper upstairs over the new store. He had 16 bins of cookies with five or six pounds of cookies in a box.

The old Post Office was on the right hand-side. Great Uncle Ernest had the longest term as Post Master than any man in New York State. I believe he was Post Master for 42 years until my father took over. Ernest had the first car in Oak Hill and he had the first TV in Oak Hill. He got it in '38 or '40. It was all snow; it was more snow than picture.

During the war some of the stores would do black market but he wouldn't do it and the boarding houses and resorts needed sugar and he wouldn't sell it. The one thing he could do was put in beer, wine, but he didn't want to be competition to Angie and Gertie next door at DeWitt's Hotel. This hurt his business.

I was born in 1932. I started working there when I was 13. I stocked shelves and waited on customers. I played for a while on the Oak Hill Baseball Team. The team played 19 years against 22 different towns. Ernest sponsored the team. He bet a little on the side, secretly. They played over by where the field is now and a homerun was in the creek.

My brother and I were offered the business. We talked for

several hours and we decided that it didn't have a chance to survive. As my dad knew and predicted the first supermarket would be in Greenville and everyone would go there.

Willard Elsbree served as a college professor in Ohio. He returns every summer to the home where he was born and raised in Preston Hollow. Often he can be found sitting on his porch overlooking Elsbree Field, named in memory of his grandfather.

I remember the Negro Leagues Brooklyn Royal Giants played here in Preston Hollow. I saw the game. I think the Giants won. One of the players played the role of a clown with a rubber cigar and all that stuff. The game with the Giants was in the mid- 30's, I'm guessing.

Bob Dingman was a local boy and his farm was on the road between Cooksburg and Oak Hill. My sister went to school with Mary Mitchell, who married Bob. He died quite young. He was one of the standard baseball players. Guy Dingman had a store down here, in Preston Hollow, a barber shop and he used to cut my hair. Anyway, Guy was a pitcher who had good days and bad days.

Charlie lives down the street here. His sister Nancy Lake got my brother to write the account of the team. My brother Hugh died in 2004, he was 100 and he had an excellent memory. Hugh taught at Dartmouth and headed the reference section in the Library of Congress.

Leo Ford's widow married Charlie Radick, Sr. and she's living in Florida now, she's about 95. Ernest Ford and my father were merchants together. My father had the store here in Preston Hollow. It's a bookstore today.

I remember Oak Hill in the 30's and then the 40's. The Hunts used to live in Ives' farm. Dr. Simmons used to live in Oak Hill. The Peck family was there. Jack DeWitt had a sister named Pat and she died young of TB. Tracy Tompkins was the electrician who lived in Oak Hill. I remember Hall and Burnett's Store was failing but Ford's Store was still operating and the Creamery and DeWitt's Hotel, which was mostly a bar. Woodie's served ice cream and you got film developed there. My sister used to take piano lessons from Mrs. Pratt. Alfred Burnett, he always came to ball games, he was scorekeeper and he followed the team around.

Roy Brandow was one of those people who had means, but I never knew what he did. He seemed to like baseball and he often was there and they commandeered him to umpire. He had one daughter and she died when in high school, a very sad thing. He's buried over in Manorkill.

After many years of running the Glen Royal, Anson Schumann is a well-known and popular figure around Oak Hill.

I was born in Brooklyn, in Greenwood, in 1934 and moved to Preston Hollow in 1946 with mother and stepfather. I worked on a farm when I was 13 or 14 for $5 a week. Plus I got three meals a day, meat, potatoes, the whole deal. Haying, milking cows, plowing, the whole schmeer. I went to school in Middleburgh and went into the Marines and then to the Korean

War. When I got out I moved to Long Island because that's where my mother was. I lived in Levittown and then moved back to Preston Hollow in '76 and then got the store in '78 and moved to Oak Hill in the early '90s.

That store, it was always Woodie's Glen Royal. When I was a kid I went with Woodie's daughter. It had newspapers, comic books, pin ball machine, pool table and more when we were kids.

I always wanted the store and when I was retired from the carpenters union I was able to buy it. I put on the addition on the right. I had it from '78 until '95. It was the only place in town then and people started their day there and ended their day there. I opened at 5:00 a.m. and stayed until nine at night, except in the winter when we stopped at eight o'clock. It was open seven days a week. It never closed. It made money and was a success.

Now I live in the trailer park. I used to live across from the Twelve Tribes, up Route 81, on the hill. I put that house up there. I miss the restaurant. I miss the people. The whole town used to come in, everybody in this town knows me, it was family. I had three heart attacks, two strokes, open heart surgery and cancer all since I was 50.

There was no work in Oak Hill. This was the poverty area of Greene County, this area here. Most of these little towns were self-sufficient, either you worked in the town or you owned the business. The big business came and broke down the economic system. Progress eliminated the little town, either you were big or you got out. I definitely see this town improving though. People are coming into the area because they ain't making any more land.

Anna Hamm today lives contentedly not far from her place of birth. Her father was a farmer in Freehold and her mother served the area for many years as a schoolteacher.

I was born in 1930. I lived outside Oak Hill. I was born in Freehold, right near here. Then later on we lived on a farm where Cahill Road is, less than a mile up, we owned the first farm on the right. My father was Alfred Bullivant, originally from East Windham.

My mother was Elvira Bullivant. She taught in where the museum is now in Durham Center Museum, before I was born. Then my mother taught in Oak Hill in the early 30's. My mother taught until 1970 and then she retired. She died in 1993. She was almost 90.

My best friend was Shirley Burnett, Alfred and Elizabeth's daughter, and she lived next door to the Parsonage until they moved across the street. I spent a lot of time in their house. We spent a lot of time in each others' homes. We were always happy. Kids played a lot together, which they don't too much now. It didn't take much to make us happy, I guess.

I spent a lot of time down at the Lounsbury's. Betty Lounsbury was my good friend too. Mr. Lounsbury had a barber shop and the living quarters were beyond. We spent a lot of time in

Hall and Burnett's store, too. Shirley Burnett, her grandfather owned it. I spent a lot of time in that place. Calvin Burnett was her grandfather. We'd walk down to Ford's Store two or three times a day just to have something to do.

They used to have card parties at the IOOF Hall where the Oak Hill Kitchen is now. Everybody went to play different types of cards and sometimes kids would go. There were so many nice places in Oak Hill, I think. It was livelier than it is now.

I remember one time I was going up to the Central School, it must have been the early 40's, and we had a bad blizzard and for three weeks my father took us to school in a horse and sleigh.

There were several places that sold gas in Oak Hill: Lounsbury's, Woodie's and Hyatt Field's Garage. Now there's one in the township and there used to be three in the town.

The renovation, in Oak Hill today, is good. Years ago you knew everybody who lived in every house but now you don't. I think it's good to see that somebody is doing something. Years ago people didn't have a lot of money but they kept their house looking nice. They didn't have junk all over. That trailer park over in Oak Hill, you know, it kills me. Maybe they didn't have paint but they didn't have junk all over it.

I hope the Twelve Tribes do well in the Oak Hill Kitchen. They had such a fuss when they came. They seem like good people. Their kids aren't vandalizing the place. I hope it works out. One thing that hurts them is having their Sabbath on

Saturday. They take care of things and they are conscientious. The kids aren't running around screaming.

In my day the worst that any child ever did was get caught smoking and that was bad. I remember we cut one cigarette in half so that Alfred wouldn't miss it. Today I can't understand why they would want to get involved with narcotics. I think we lived in the best of times, although we didn't have much. I guess I'm happy I lived when I did.

Burt Mattice could frequently be found holding court at Oak Hill's Internally Gratefull Café. Sadly, Burt passed away in December, 2006.

I was born in '23. I came to Oak Hill for a job and then just stayed. Originally from Stanford, New York. I came here in '45 to run Lounsbury's store. I came out of the service on November 15, I was married on December 2 and by January 1 I was over here in business. About three weeks later I woke up, pinched myself and wondered 'what have I done?'

When I came here they had Ford's Store. I went in there and Ernest, Leo Ford, they introduced me to different guys that came in: Tracy Tompkins, there was Les Wade and Alfred Burnett. The store on the upper end there, Hall and Burnett's, that was operating too. We had two stores in town and then we had five gas stations where you could get gas, unbelievable, unbelievable.

I was gonna run that store, take over that business for a

guy, but it didn't work out and the guy wanted me to go to Middleburgh. So Tracy Tompkins and them talked me into staying so I stayed and carried on.

The first place we lived was the old Schoolhouse up on Schoolhouse Hill Road. It was so damned cold up there you couldn't stand it. When the wind blowed the rugs floated right on the floor. I worked from the store there in Lounsbury's at the bottom of Schoolhouse Hill Road. Willet Lounsbury, he was a barber, he had a barber shop there. I remember every Thursday night there they had card games there. He sold Frigidaire appliances there.

Folks, they were pretty religious around here. Everybody went to church on Sunday and the kids went to Sunday School. All the good Christians lived up there on Christian Hill. The Tripps lived there next to their store and the Parsonage was there, the church was there. All the people from the church lived up there. Ever since I remember, it was always called Christian Hill because all the good Christians lived there in that part of town and all the heathens lived down on this end. They had the idea that they were working for God but my theory is that God don't pay my bills and when he pays my bills then I'll work for him.

We started the fire company in 1945. East Durham had the only one in the town and so they couldn't handle it all and after the war all the fellas started them up in all the little hamlets. Ours was next to the funeral home. Potter used to own it and then he died and Cunningham bought it. He didn't need the garage for the hearse and all because he had another place down in Greenville. So we used the garage for the fire truck.

Stiefel was some fire. We had it alarmed and all but all them chemicals in there caused it to go up quick. The night crew in there tried to fight it themselves at first. We were lucky we saved the buildings next to it, but we did, thanks to the crick.

Charlie Newman had a sister and a house and a horse, a couple of cows, chickens there in a barn and he couldn't get to the barn 'less he crossed a bridge. There was a stream running there. Old 'rubber boots Charlie', he wore them old barn boots day and night. He read that *Wall Street Journal* very religiously. He died and then Howard Poultney bought the property and he turned it into the trailer park.

I was in a band and every Saturday night we played a square dance somewheres around here. The Stardusters was the name of the band back then. Well, at times there was six of us. When we wound up there was just three of us playing boarding houses and stuff like that. I had the car loaded with drums and I had two or three other kids that ride with me. Made good money too, met a lot of wonderful people. Played nights and worked days. We made $50 dollars a night. That was good money. We played from nine up 'til eleven or twelve o'clock, go home and go to sleep, and get up at five and go to work.

Leo Ford built the house on the other side of the park here.

Delamater, he was the old photographer, lived in what they say was the Tremain family house. I'd like to know what happened to his old glass types. He moved away to Medusa probably in the 40's. I don't know just when he died.

Leslie Wade. He was a good old guy. His brother was Donald. Les Wade was an amateur photographer. He'd go around on weekends taking pictures. He painted pictures. You'd give him a photograph and he'd make it into a painting. His wife Mary wound up in a nursing home. She was a great old girl, too. She always had a story to tell. Jokes, she loved jokes and the dirtier the better.

He used to come over and eat supper with us. He used to leave the back light on, that was his guiding light home. He was going blind; nobody really realized just how blind he was getting. He'd never admit it. Then one night he didn't show up to eat. Every so often he'd go down to Woodie's and get some ice cream and bring it up and have ice cream after supper.

One night he didn't show up. Then my wife, said, "What happened to Pop? He didn't show up for supper." His light wasn't on. I called down to Woodie and he wasn't down there. I went over to the house, didn't see him and hollered, yelled and he didn't answer me. So I came out. I went around to the window of the woodhouse door there, and there he hung. Hung up off the step ladder. He left a note and he always said this, that he wasn't going to be dependent on nobody. He didn't want to leave Oak Hill. Then he up and did this.

It was a hell of a lot better in the old days. Back then, we were all friends and friendly and nobody bothered with anybody else's business and today everybody is trying to run everyone's business. People resent it that don't say a hell of a lot about it but they resent it.

Oak Hill was a whole lot better back then, a lot better, it was unbelievable back then. Today everybody's trying to screw each other, it's true, you're gonna find that out. If you had a problem everybody helped each other. If we needed a hand we helped each other. We'd go in each other's shop and took what we needed. Money never changed hands, we just helped each other and that's the way we operated. Our buildings was never locked, our house was never locked until these last few years. But, I gotta outlive my father, whether I do or not I don't know. He was 87.

Harriet Rasmussen was raised in Cairo but her fondest memories were of her frequent visits to her Aunt Elizabeth and Uncle Alfred Burnett in Oak Hill. Today she lives in nearby Greenville.

Alfred Tripp was born in 1807 and he married Mariah Utter. They both died at the brick house. Alfred gave the store to his son Isaac, we called him Ike, and he sold it and it was Hall and Burnett's then. Calvin Burnett had worked as a clerk. The Tripp sisters married Hall and Burnett in 1900 on the same day. They took over the store and got it paid for by 1919. Byron Hall was one of the store owners and the other owner was Alfred's father, Calvin Burnett. They married the two youngest Tripp sisters, Hattie and Carrie, so they were brothers-in-law. Carrie and Calvin lived in the brick house with Isaac Tripp and the rest of the family and Byron and Hattie lived in a house at the top of Christian Hill. Ike died in 1941.

Alfred Tripp Burnett was born July 25, 1901. He was the son of Calvin Burnett and Carrie. He married my mother's sister, Elizabeth Griffin. He was the Uncle that to me was like a second father. Alfred Burnett was the only grandson in the Tripp family. There were two other grandchildren, both girls, and they were both older than him. Uncle Alfred's mother Carrie was the youngest girl. He was the only boy, with a lot of aunts to give him attention.

He went to Cornell for a year or so and might have taken animal husbandry or something but he didn't like it. He was painting at the Parsonage and I think that started his painting days. He and Leslie Wade were a team and they did almost all of the boarding houses, Shepherd's and Balsam Shade. They started with one building and they kept putting buildings on and they painted them.

My maiden name was Abrams and I grew up in Cairo but my dad grew up in Oak Hill, and he and Alfred were friends and they started going with the two girls. Mother and father were married in '21 and Aunt Elizabeth and Uncle Alfred were married in '25, the year I was born.

Alfred was a mild tempered man and loved to read. He was a great reader and he had books. Book cases here and book cases there. He was a good ballplayer and he played for the ball team. I remember going to Maplecrest to watch the ball team and Maplecrest at that time was a big resort area. He used to shoot pool down at Woodie's store. He bowled the highest score at the bowling alley. I remember when he died suddenly on Dec 25, 1970 at his home in Oak Hill.

Aunt Elizabeth didn't think you had to do the dishes. Uncle Alfred is doing the dishes while two young girls, my sister and I, are doing nothing, it wasn't right. At her house it was like a vacation. Next to my mother, we loved this Aunt, and that went on 'til the day she died.

I remember my brother Charles Abrams loved to stay with Aunt Elizabeth and Uncle Alfred during the summer so he could play on that baseball team. He is seven years younger than I and his days in Oak Hill came after mine but he has his own fond memories of his times there.

Byron had two elderly sisters, Annie and Lou, who were spinsters and they lived on one side of Alfred and Elizabeth's house. They dressed in Victorian times in '29 or '30 and they shared the house. There was an outside privy and you went outside the back and there was a long walk. In those days they kept chambers too. In the back of the kitchen where my Aunt lived there was a big open room, we called it a mud room. When I stop to think about it, how primitive it all was.

Aunt Elizabeth (to us Aunt Ebbie) would come to Cairo, usually in a big Studebaker, to take us to Oak Hill. Often Aunt Hattie Hall and Aunt Carrie Burnett came along for the ride. They were two little old sisters and we were two little five and six year old sisters. Whenever I ride past the flat stretch by the Ives farm it takes me back to those days. When we came to that stretch we always knew we were getting near the house.

My Aunt used to go to Catskill in the Studebaker and on the way back she would stop in Cairo and we could always tell if she had been there-she would leave us in the buffet drawer a Hershey bar. Now, you know one of those Hershey bars had the little squares in it and we didn't see a Hershey bar unless she had been there and that was a few times a year. But, I think about it today, kids take so much for granted. We used to, my sister and I, divide up those little squares, one for each day, and make that go. Kids have no concept of it. Why would they have a concept of it? People in my generation are savers and hate to throw away food and that comes from that. Even though now there's no need for it.

Ken Mabey's appreciation of Oak Hill is based on both his personal experience growing up there and his devotion to history.

I was born in '37. I was born in Freehold and moved to Oak Hill in '49 or '50 and before that was in Oak Hill frequently because my Aunt Margaret lived there, my father's sister. Hugh Hayes was a plumber who married her. He was a nice person who had more then a little drinking problem.

Karen and Bob McAll's house, which is just west of the icicle house, was where my Aunt lived and across the street was where my grandmother lived. That would be around 1948. I lived in my grandparents' place and I lived in my Aunt Margaret's place too. My parents were divorced and my mother remarried and moved to New Jersey and I came to Oak Hill with my father and stepmother.

It was even in the 1940's that Oak Hill probably was already declining. The real heyday of Oak Hill was probably in the mid 19th century. The decline probably started by the early 1900's. A lot of it had to do with the decline of agriculture. A lot had to do with the supply and need of the local farmer. You didn't travel huge distances. By the time the car came out you were still going from one local small town to another, like Cornwallville to Oak Hill and to Cairo. As cars improved it was easy to get to great distances.

When Al Bryant started his store he had been in nearby Westerlo. That was just a small store like all these other small stores around here. In the 1950's or 60's, then he went down to Greenville and they made that large supermarket. I graduated in '55. I think it happened right around 1960 or so.

Pete Cooke was quiet but interesting and he loved baseball. He managed the town baseball team. And Robby, his son, was big on the team. Robby Cooke and I were very close. We played ball together and went out with girls together. They had at one time a very good baseball team. Junior Ives played 2nd base, he was a pretty good player. They were originally the Oak Hill Plowboys. I played my last year in high school, that would be 1955, I played short stop in high school and on the town team I played 2nd or 3rd.

I remember going to Hall and Burnett's, Alfred Burnett was his son, when I was a little kid. It looked much like it is today. They sold general merchandise and they weren't very busy. It wasn't a going concern as it probably was in the earlier days. Because by this time people had cars and could go elsewhere. There was an elderly woman in the store and it was very quiet. They had a few customers. Hall and Burnett's closed down sometime in the early 1940's. Even Woodie's sold some groceries and Ford's too.

Leo ran Ford's Store quite vigorously for some time. Leo died young, reasonably young, in his 50's. Glen Hulbert eventually became postmaster, replacing Leo. Leo's wife was Ruth. They had three children, George and Lionel, and Kay was a year older than me and she passed away, a beautiful girl, a nice girl.

Helen and her husband Woodie were quite a fixture in the community. That was the village hangout, not only for kids but for the older generation too. Old men would come in and shoot pool. It was kind of neat to listen to and I developed an appreciation for older people. Harold Woodruff was quite a guy. I remember the treat he invented, called the What Not. Vanilla ice cream, marshmallows, nuts and a lot of other stuff. The idea was, What's in it? What's not in it!

When I was in college I'd come home to hunt. We used to go with Woodie and there was always a party of us. At one time this was part of my culture. Today I'm too tender-hearted to hunt.

I painted Brooks Atkinson's house a couple of times. He was a nice elderly man, very bright and interesting to talk to. I talked to him once, about the first time I painted his house. We somehow talked about the people in the area. He said, "The intellectual curiosity of the people around here is not very great but their sense of decency is very high." He was the type of guy that was stimulated by intellectual things.

Carol Cooke lives today on the same farm on which she was raised on the western end of Oak Hill.

My father was Fred Cooke and a lot of people called him Pete. Mary Dingman, next door, called him Pete and it just stuck. I'm a third generation on this farm. My mother was Margaret Goff and it was her parents, Rhoba and Ed Goff, who started this farm. My grandparents came to Oak Hill in the 1920's, I think. This house is well over two hundred years old. This was a very self-sufficient farm. There were orchards and grape vineyards, all kinds of fruits, they grew lots of crops, barley, wheat, nuts and they had chickens, cows, ducks, all sorts of animals.

My father was a carpenter. When they moved off the farm they moved an old schoolhouse up across the street, the next place up, and made it into a house. He moved it from East Durham; I think it was in the 40's. It was demolished and made room for a new house. He was Deputy Sheriff for the County.

Pete was born in 1912. He was instrumental in starting the Oak Hill Baseball Team. He was the manager for quite a few years. He played in the Mountain League. They had a lot of fans. Go up Schoolhouse Hill and you bear to the right and it was off on the left there, that's where they first played. Pete died in '82 and he ran the farm until then.

My mother was Town Clerk for 35 years in this house. They had a town meeting once a month. My father's brother was Town Supervisor at one time. An opening came up for Town Clerk so she ran for it every two years. She retired around 1983. She died in '92.

In the 1940's and 50's it was idyllic living in Oak Hill. Now looking at what kids are exposed to and all that it was a wonderful way to grow up. We had friends and horses. We went riding together. We could get into mischief but nothing like they are exposed to today. Anne Field was my friend, Hyatt Field was her father. He had the garage on the edge of town.

Horse shows were a big thing, every summer we'd go to Poultney's Flats. We'd go on trail rides. There wasn't the traffic in the road. You came home from school and had chores to do but then we'd ride.

In the first grade I had Mrs. Bullivant. Mrs. Bullivant had red hair, a feisty thing. They were strict, they weren't there to be your friend, they were there to teach you. You were not passed ahead if you didn't know the material. You don't deserve it if you don't work for it. High school was fun but it was hard work too.

I went to Durham for grade school and Greenville for high school. There were about 20 in my class. It was a fantastic school with small classes and dedicated teachers and there were no discipline problems. They were allowed to use corporal punishment and it didn't hurt anybody. If you got sent to the principle you were ashamed. I graduated in '58.

We didn't rely on material things that much for entertainment. Things weren't important. If you worked six months for something, you got it and you took care of it. Today you need something new every five minutes.

Our neighbors got TV before we did. A couple of times a month we'd go over for a spaghetti dinner and watch TV. Then we got one and it was a novelty and we'd put the trays in front of the TV. We only got one channel, I think it was six and we saw *The Ed Sullivan Show*, westerns, the news. But after a while we went back to eating at the kitchen table. It was a big deal; they had to run a wire across the road to an antenna. We never got good reception.

I could remember when we got a bathroom and that was a big thing. They had the electric milk machine and before that he did it by hand. Twice a day, every day, he had 20-25 cows. If the electricity was out everybody was out there milking cows. I used to have to feed calves with a bottle with a nipple on it and they had supplement. I had to feed the pigs and worked a big garden, hoe and weed. I helped mom preserve the stuff with canning. If we wanted vegetables we went down the basement and got it.

Ford's Store was the main store and the Post Office was there. Dad and I would go and pick up the mail. Then we'd go to DeWitt's Hotel next door. I had a soda and dad had a beer. People would congregate and talk, play cards, darts and dominoes. The bathroom was at the top of the stairs in DeWitt's Hotel. The bar was in the first room when you went in the side door by what is now the parking lot. I think the living quarters were on the other side of the stairs.

Lounsbury was an appliance store then. My grandfather bought the first refrigerator that was delivered after World War II and we were still using that refrigerator in 1995. It was a little rusty but it still worked. My grandparents' Monarch Stove still works.

Transportation made it so easy to get someplace else. The people traveled more into Cairo or Greenville. The gas was cheap. A lot of farms closed. There is no industry here. Very little to really keep people.

I worked for Stiefel for 38 years. I started part time in college in the library and I worked in the personnel office. I worked in New York City for ten years and then Connecticut for five years. Stiefel manufactures skin care products, medicinal. It started in Germany, went to Preston Hollow and then to Oak Hill. I would say they moved down to the village in the late 40's and early 50's. The Creamery became Stiefel's soap factory. George Ford was Treasurer for a while, Leo's son.

One of my duties was moving the whole library, all of the books, and the night before it burned down the truck had come and moved. The place burned to the ground. Stiefel was on Route 145 and that day all the records went over there and that night the fire happened. I don't think that it was ever determined how it happened. Now they're transferring people to North Carolina, research and development.

We had a lot of local boys over there in Vietnam and some of them didn't come back. We were more patriotic about it. We would never consider using the flag for a bonfire. John Dedek lost his life in Vietnam. He lived up the street, the first one on the left. He was 19 or 20. He was a marine. He was from Oak Hill. Jerry Adolphi, he was in the Marines and he lived up Lee Road.

Ethan is often found at the Twelve Tribes' Oak Hill Kitchen where he performs the duties of the owner.

I was born in Newport, Vermont in 1965. I joined the Twelve Tribes in 1978 along with my parents and two sisters. I wasn't too crazy about it at the time. I was just starting high school and there were some teachers who thought I had a lot of potential to be a rock musician.

Anyway, first we went to northeast Vermont and later Boston. I went through about five years in the community and there were adults that taught me things and touched me deep, through their love. There was something that I really treasured about this life in the community. On the other hand, I was interested in the real world. My two sisters adjusted more easily, they were ten and seven. We had no snowmobile, no TV or any of those things that young people like. I had relatives who offered me a home if I was willing to leave the community. I actually left for a short time, 24 hours. I was 19. I rode about 40 miles west of Boston on a bicycle but I realized that there was a lot I was leaving behind and there was nothing to go to.

When I first started out I was very interested in farming. At around 18 I had a desire to learn carpentry and I spent the next 18 years learning about construction. I got married in '87. I have seven children. Now I spend a lot of time teaching the children of the community to play music.

The Twelve Tribes was started by a group of people believing in the idea of giving up possessions. They wanted to be 100 percent about what they were reading in the *Bible*. Some people were content with just going to church on Sunday and so these people were like the first disciples, they lived together in a community. They were just trying to get back to the way it was when Christ was raised from the dead. Now it's in Germany, France, Spain, Brazil, Argentina, Canada and the U.S. It's been around now about 35 years and there are a few thousand people in it. There are struggles, though, growth pains. As we expand and go to different places some people have to go to other places to help. We're stretched a little thin.

Anyway, back in the 90's we were living in Boston, about 120 of us. We were starting to have large families and we began to think that we needed a farm. Around Boston everything was going from a million or a million and a half and it wasn't in our grasp. Then we found a 100 acre farm in Oak Hill that we could afford.

We built the woodshop in the first two or three years. In Boston we were a construction company. So we said, "Let's set up a woodshop to support the jobs of the construction company. We will have an income while we are at home with our families."

My first impression of Oak Hill was a quiet place with not much happening. We had a couple of weddings here about eight years ago and I thought it was very refreshing to come to Oak Hill but the town didn't seem like there was a lot going on. The café helps us to meet a lot of people in the area now.

Controversy got stirred up when we first came to town and there were people who came to town and spread lies that we are bad people and we are a cult. There were people who left the community and never gave their whole heart and it was a torture chamber of the flesh for them and they may have started the rumors. The way we deal with it is that we tell people, "Come and ask us about us, don't just listen to rumors."

We value moral standards of times past. We are trying to get back to what's right. We don't want to go with the flow of the world. We feel that the world is going towards destruction. In Revelations it says that the world is going to become more and more evil. Moral standards are slowly being eroded away. It's gradual and subtle, that's how the devil works. In the last days men will be lovers of pleasure instead of lovers of God and they'll call evil good and good evil.

When I was a boy my father would pull me away from the TV and put me to work and now that's called an evil thing.

Now I look back and say my father loved me and he didn't want me to grow up as a lazy bum. I had a purpose as a teenager and I valued and loved it. It was hard at times but I am so glad.

My hope is that my children will come with me and trust me. They are not held here. Some young people leave and come back. My daughter has never been on a date, never kissed anybody, never held anybody's hand. There will come a time when she meets someone and she will hold hands and if they fall in love and be betrothed then on the wedding day they'll have the first kiss. Parents have to teach their children about their sexuality and I talk to my children and it's the most Godly thing that we have.

A lot of our decisions to move people are for their own benefit. There was a young man who was going nuts in Oak Hill because he was a people person and so we sent him to Boston. Every week married couples get together and talk about social issues in the community life and the women are greatly involved and women decide how to make it a home and a family. They have a lot of the wisdom that we need.

Part of our commitment is that our lives are not our own, it's for the benefit of the spiritual nation. There are a lot of demands on our lives and we want to give up self lives. We want to be self-less. We have a council and we get together. In New York State we have four or five communities and once a month two or three men from each community will meet and discuss what's going on in each community and see what the needs are. They suggested I move to Ithaca and help a café get started there. I had the freedom to say I really feel like I would like to stay and that I want to push this café ahead here in Oak Hill. We listen to one another, listen to the least. I was taught how to be a leader by being sensitive to others, by listening.

William Winans lives on the far eastern end of Oak Hill in a house he built over half a century ago.

I was born 1913. I was born in Preston Hollow and moved to Potter Hollow in 1922. In 1932 I was working for a fellow by Oak Hill and we were doing a little carpentry work on the road from Medusa to Norton Hill. Medusa had burned. We came over to the back street and met a carpenter who was building the Ford house. My father's uncle and I worked for him. We worked for 26 years and I did a lot of work in this area. I probably built all told about 100 houses in this area.

Alfred Burnett played for the Sodbusters some. Hugh Elsbree was 3rd base. I saw when they played the House of David. These colored teams and teams like that, they were professionals, there's no getting around it. My brother's name was Charles and I think he was an outfielder.

That building in the back off 81 is Elm Rest. I helped build that building in '38 or '39. She sold it, I think in the 60's, I'm not sure. Hyatt Field was her second husband. She could take 125 people. She had a good kitchen. I think she sold the whole works for $90,000.

The 30's was about the time I was getting started in carpentry. At that time it was pretty much a farming section with the exception of people who came up to the resorts in the summer.

Today Eugene Kellam lives peacefully in a small house by a large pond just a few miles away from Oak Hill.

William Henry Kellam, that was my father. They lived up around Loudonville. My dad worked for the Shakers and my mother did too. They were up around where Albany airport is. My dad worked for them for quite a few years in the teens or somewhere. They were like the Mormons. I don't know what his chores were, I guess he was just a handyman. He more or less did odd jobs all over, more or less keeping the property up and all that stuff.

I was born in just the start of '24, Jan 8. When I was born we were living over in East Greenbush over in Rensselaer County across the river. My dad was working over there and I was born in Albany Medical Center. My grandfather and grandmother had a farm out here called the old Saint John Farm. I don't know how old I was when we moved down Oak Hill way, near my Grandmother. She lived down below Oak Hill.

I guess my sister, Helen, probably told you my dad was killed in a mill accident. We were very young, I was about four and she was about three and a half years younger than I am. My dad didn't have no insurance and my mother, Mae, lost their place.

She opened a tea room and she done well. Things were pretty hard then, it was the Depression time. There were a couple of professional men in town and some didn't have no wives and they liked to go and get a cup of tea and a sandwich. So she opened up what she called a tea room and she made sandwiches and pies and cakes for sale in there. And that's how we survived.

Then she got the appointment of the telephone office and she was pretty lucky because there wasn't any telephone office in the village and she was there when it opened and there when it closed. They closed it prematurely because the dial system went in and we had the old fashioned switch board. I knew how to work it.

When somebody rang ya they rang with a hand crank. It was a complicated system but I was born with it. When there was an electrical storm there was fire coming out of it all over the place. It was quite an interesting piece of machinery. There were a lot of people listening in on other people, a party line. I was probably 10 or 11 when I first started to help out there.

Three old men owned that house, the Anthony boys. They were a good bunch, though, and for bachelors they loved kids pretty well. Denny used to throw pennies all over the place and make us look for them.

My mother's maiden name was Lounsbury. There's a bunch of Lounsburys around Oak Hill and they're all relatives of mine. My uncle, he lived right across the street from us when we was in Oak Hill, when my mother ran the telephone office. He had a gas station and a barber shop there. I had lost my dad at that time and I always thought a lot of my uncle. He was my mother's brother. His name was Willet and he never took his boys to do something what he didn't ask me to go. It was quite nice; he was kind of a proxy dad. He cut my hair for free, never had to pay for a haircut.

Lounsbury had a billiard room in the back. I played pool since I was old enough to hold a cue stick because that's what we did for amusement when it wasn't busy. We had to give up for paying customers, though. I played with the four boys, they were my cousins. They had some quite interesting poker games going on over there. Talk about a smoke-filled room! If second hand smoke could kill people it should have killed us a long time ago. They played poker half the night over there. Willet died young of liver cancer and so did his wife.

We had three stores, what they used to call Woodie's, then there's Hall and Burnett's and then Ford's Store. We had Dr. Ralph Stevens and we had Dr. Simmons, I guess he was retired. Dr. Romney was the veterinarian. We had Clark DeWitt as a veterinarian. Everybody had cows and horses. You needed veterinarians more than you did M.D.'s.

From the day I was 16 I never lived at home. I went to work on the farms. I worked on the old Cooke farm up the road there just above where the Twelve Tribes own that land. I worked for Pete and Margaret.

I worked for Ed Goff for a while, Margaret's father. Ed was a sort of funny guy and he went and got a school house that they abandoned, The Wright Street School, and put it on his property and made it into a house. He took all the telephone wires down for about two miles. They gave it up because the school district centralized and a lot of them little schools closed. It's right above the farm. I helped him make it into the house. Unbeknown to everybody he took a lot of telephone wires down with it. He knocked out all the low wires, he done it at night. He got in trouble for that. He used to drink quite a little. He was a character, that Ed Goff.

I used to get the fires going for the Methodist Church. It was a nice little church. The Sunday School was an hour before church at ten in the morning. Carl Ratsch was our Sunday School teacher, not all the time, but most of the time. I went to get the church open for Sunday sermons. I heard a ding, ding, ding, ding and I turned around and there was this skunk. He got a jar on his head and every time he took a step he banged it on the cement floor. I was always told how to handle a problem like that, ya lift them by the tail and keep their paws off the ground to keep 'em from stinkin'. He had his tail straight up in the air and I grabbed it. I took the jar off his head and he didn't squirt me but I don't trust them buggers.

We had all eight grades in one room. At four years old I wanted to go to school. They kept sending me home but my mother said to them, "Every time I turn my back he's up there." I used to set in a lot of classes up there. We had two teachers, and man, it was pretty confusing with two teachers talking at the same time. If you were distracted it was very understandable.

Baseball was big back then. I remember them playing the Negro Giants. It was at Preston Hollow. I thought they beat 'em. I thought they beat 'em but I'm not positive. I remember attending it because somebody took me to it. They had some real good players there. Guy Dingman was a good pitcher. He had long arms that reached halfway down to the batter. Bob Dingman married Mary, who was the schoolteacher.

Pete Cooke liked his beer pretty well and I used to baby sit for Robby, his son. Robby come down and he said to me, "What's pa doing in the manger up there?" I said, "I guess he had a little too much to drink." He said, "You think we could put him in the wheelbarrow and bring him to the house?" and that's what we done.

There were two boys, Lee and Dabner, and I remember Dabner being on the back of the sleigh with me. He was on the back and I ran into the tree. My grandmother was watching and she said, "You hit that tree with such force I thought you killed that boy." I was laying belly gut and Dabner was kneeling on the back with his hands on the rail, I crashed into the tree and it stopped quite suddenly and he hit his head. It was a wonder he wasn't hurt quite seriously. It was a horse chestnut tree that belonged to my uncle who had the barbershop there. We were going too fast, I think. We used to be able to use the public highway for sleigh runs in my day 'cause there weren't a lot of cars, there were a lot of sleighs and buggies.

We had a couple of suicides in Oak Hill. Horatio Hale committed suicide in the early 1940's, 1940 or 1941. He lived on the other side of 81 from the Cooke farm and he had an older house. He shot himself. I was working on the farm down below. I was milking the cows and the undertaker came in, Lee Cunningham, and I said, "You ain't gonna get me into something that I don't want to do." Then he smiled and I knew what it was even before he told me. He wanted me to help him carry out the body bag because they couldn't get a vehicle in there. I don't like that kind of thing at all, he put a shotgun under his chin. I don't want any part of it. Don't have the stomach for it.

We had a dentist called Dr. Hunt but one time there was a dentist moved into town from Canada. I remember going up the stairs. He didn't have a drill that run by electricity he had a drill that went by foot power. He pumped it with his foot and that made the drill go around. No Novocain, no nothing. But fortunate for me, before he got back to me they arrested him for practicing medicine without a license. The goldarn filling fell out.

The Pratt Place was next to Tracy Tompkins' place where my sister Helen lives now. The Laraways lived in the column house across the street. I remember the Creamery before it burned down. They had some quite nice houses back in the old days. One thing I liked was they had a porch on them. I like a house with a porch.

I knew the proprietors of three stores. I think I spent more time in Ford's Store because there was always a checker game going on or something going on all the while and it was entertaining. The other store was just the opposite, there was two old guys running it, they called it Hall and Burnett's. They were sort of older people back then. They were all business; they had a genuine old-fashioned store with all the fixtures in it. I'm trying to think where my mother sent me more. I think I was sent up to Hall and Burnett's as much as Ford. I used to go to Ford's often because the Post Office was there. Then Woodie, from the Glen Royal, used to take me fishing. He went trout fishing and he'd take me because he felt sorry for me because I didn't have a dad.

Once, I rode my bicycle after somebody told me that there was a fire in Medusa. It burned quite a few more houses then I thought it would. It was something you don't see very often. Fire trucks were there. They didn't have very good fire fighting equipment back then; they didn't have very good pumps on them. They did the best they could. I stood up on the hill near my friend Porter Wright's house. It must have been on a Saturday or Sunday. I saw half the village of Medusa burned down.

I think Oak Hill went down hill eventually when the two stores went out of business. When the local stores went and the farmers didn't do their business locally. It changed the whole thing of the town. Well, I think they got a little rebound of the places. They are bringing it back to the way it was. The lower end of the village was the worse. Today these old houses are harder than blitzen to heat.

All in all though, I liked the good old days a lot better than today. I think a lot of it is the social part of it more than anything. Everybody was so congenial. Even after we were married we went from one house to the next and played cards and games that today is no more. Back then you didn't have to worry about entertainment. You didn't need the goldarn TV to set and watch all the while or a computer. Back then we didn't even have electricity. We read with an oil lamp. So folks say to me, "You wouldn't want to move back to the old days with all the hardships you had to endure." And I say, "It wouldn't bother me a bit." Except I wouldn't care for the outdoor john at my age. I liked the old days. I liked the horse and wagon. Doggone it, you know that even though there was a lot of hardship and we didn't have the lush cars and computers of today, people were a lot friendlier.

Donald Lounsbury lives with his wife, Loretta, in the house where they have resided for over 50 years.

My mother told me they put a new bridge in Oak Hill the year I was born. I was born August 23, 1927. My father was Willet Lounsbury, he lived around Oak Hill most of the time but was originally from Loudonville near Albany, and my mother was Florence. He started a barbershop but they got the Frigidaire franchise and they sold refrigerators there too. The men used to come in two nights a week and play cards and shoot pool. I had three brothers and one sister. We slept up over the barber shop and a good many mornings there was snow up to the windowsill of the second floor.

The pool table was up in back and the men played cards over in the corner. He started in 1931 and in 1936 they sold one refrigerator, pretty rough year. Willet died at 43 years old of cancer. He smoked cigars; maybe he smoked two packs of cigarettes in his whole life. I think it was in 1947 when he died. When we got married we lived in a three room apartment upstairs.

Everybody knew everybody back then and Cal Burnett and Byron Hall ran the upper store. They didn't have too much stuff. They were both good men, they married the Tripp sisters. They had money. I mowed the lawn for them and I had to mow a path out to behind the barn and someone told me that Cal Burnett was not allowed to smoke in the house and he would walk on that path out to by the crick and smoke.

Loretta lived on a farm. One night she was riding her horse, Tony, to round up the cows and bring them in. A bolt of lightening struck her and the horse. She stayed in the saddle unconscious but the horse finished rounding up the cows and then brought her home.

Alfred Burnett was Cal Burnett's son. Alfred was a good man, I never heard anyone say a word against him. He told me this himself, he said, "The day I was born it was determined I was going to go to Cornell. I went to Cornell and it didn't do me a bit of good because I like to paint houses." And that's what he did, he painted houses. Do you know where Balsam Shade is, over in Greenville? That was Alfred Burnett's wife's brother's and he and Leslie Wade spent over 50 percent of the time painting Balsam Shade. They were good painters.

Leslie Wade's son moved to Florida and he found his wife with another man and he shot and killed them both and he went to prison. Jr. Wade did. His mother and my mother got to be very good friends after my father died. Mary Wade ended up in an institution, though. Leslie Wade, Sr., killed himself. He got to be an old man and he hung himself. I was somewhere and someone come in and said, "Leslie Wade just hung himself."

Most every town had a baseball team and Preston Hollow had the best one. They had a guy named Guy Dingman pitch for them. He had the longest arms I ever seen, his arms went down to below his knees. Oak Hill had its own team but the team that everybody knew around here was the Sodbusters. They played the colored Giants from New York City and they beat 'em.

Alfred Burnett took me to Albany to see the Albany Senators and they played Connie Mack's team. I seen Connie Mack and they had Rudy York, a great first baseman. Alfred was good to everybody. They told me that he had a blood clot that hit his heart. He was in the bathroom and he fell against the door and they had an awful time getting the door open, he was 73 or 74 years old.

Then we had the undertaker. Ever hear of Stanley Potter? He had a sister Helen and a sister Marion and they laid the guys out and everything and down below Helen Hulbert's house, about three houses, was the undertaker parlor, it's an antique place now. Everybody liked Stanley Potter.

When I was in school I was hit by a car and I was put back a year. I got hit by a car up in Loudonville and we went to see a turtle that was big enough to carry someone on his back and I got hit by the car and broke my leg. The total bill was $100 and Doc Simmons got $20. Nowadays if something like that happened it would be thousands.

Oak Hill, I would say, was a typical town, nobody had any money. I mowed every lawn in Oak Hill. I swear I walked a million miles and that one that was Roy Hunt's; I got 15 cents for it. I mowed the store lawn, the church lawn. I cleaned the outhouse twice a year and they give me $2 if I emptied the outhouse. They used to buy a large bag of flour for only 89 cents. We used to go down with a wagon to draw the stuff home, now you could put a dollar's worth in your pocket.

We lived across the road from DeWitt's Hotel when we were first married. Angie and Gertie ran DeWitt's Hotel. Gertie lived with, I can't think of his name, that was the talk of the town, they lived together without being married. Herb Palmer that is what his name was. There were things going on those days too.

When I started working in the mill down here I got $28 a week for six days at Dean's Mill. You went to work at seven in the morning and worked until you made the last delivery at night. It was hard work throwing hundred pound bags. I worked there about 12 years.

I was working down at Dean's Mill when Brooks Atkinson came down one day in a big Buick station wagon and he got a bag of lye which was 60 cents at the time. I used to do the office work and he come back down and he said, "The man who waited on me gypped me out of 25 cents." Well, I wasn't going to argue with him over 25 cents so I give it to him and he went back out to his car and there laying between the seats was the quarter and he come back in and he says, "I'm sorry I did get the right change." He returned the quarter, and for a man who was worth half a million or more to care about that, but he did. He says, "I made a mistake, the quarter is right here."

When the foundries were going they had a bigger population in Oak Hill. The railroad was going to make the first trip down here at High Rock and they claim that if the railroad had succeeded Oak Hill would have been big. I remember the old iron foundry standing there and we used to play there. Jack DeWitt lived on the property and he was a very good friend of mine, he was a couple of years older. He had a sister Pat and she died of TB.

We used to go down there by the crick and we'd go down there in the morning and then we'd get home from school and we'd skate as far as Cooksburg and some years as far as High Rock in East Durham. In those days the winter was cold, a lot colder than they are now. We had a big thermometer that never got to zero the whole month of February. It stayed below zero the whole month. They put the road in the year I was born, 1927, that's what my mother told me.

I had a fish hook right in my leg; I was riding a bicycle with the hooks in my pocket. My father took me up there and I was concerned they'd ruin the hook and Dr. Stevens went out to his fishing box to get me a replacement. Dr. Stevens was a very good man. They tore down Cheritree's Inn, Dr. Stevens had an office in there, I think he was the last one to live in there. I remember Cheritree's Inn; it hasn't been down too many years.

Frank Laraway was the undertaker. His undertaking parlor was down the street on the other side of the road. Stanley Potter was there but I understood that Laraway took it over.

Elmer Felton, he was the boss of the Creamery there and he built that house there probably in the thirties. Elmer Felton was a very liked man. He come and run the Creamery but he got arthritis and he ended up in the poorhouse because of that. His wife died but Elmer Felton, everybody liked him.

Guy Mulberry moved in there years later. He owned that big farm over on 145, you know, where the Milk Run is, but he sold it and moved to Elmer's house. Because of Hattie, his wife, he had to sell it because she had bad mental spells and he had to lock her in the room. He was like a second father to me. East Durham, all them places had boarding houses so people from New York would come up. Well, he sold most of the milk to the boarding houses. He got top dollar for it because he was retailing it instead of wholesaling it.

My mother told me that when she lived in Rensselaerville that Tripp's Store was the main store and that once a year people came down and buy their winter clothes and things. Ford's was the main store when I grew up and Tripp's was run by Hall and Burnett's and they had a bit of hardware and maybe a loaf of bread or a dozen eggs. Ford's got the Post Office and when Tripp's lost the Post Office everybody went there.

The stores closed, my father's barbershop got closed because he died. People couldn't afford to keep the houses up. People died off. Then Oak Hill went down some.

We got married in 1951. First we lived in the apartment over mom's house, you know, the house on the corner going up Schoolhouse Hill, and then my brother Peter came home from the service and he got married in March and he was going to take over the business and he and his wife lived there. We moved and then we moved again over the ice cream parlor and we were freezing to death and moved here in '53.

My brother Paul was two years older than I was. He went in the Navy when he was 17 or 18, in '43 or '44, he got six weeks of basic training and he was in the South Pacific. He come home and got a farm and he thought his oldest son was going to take it over but his son wanted no part of farming, he sold the farm. He died two or three years ago, Paul. My other brother Peter run the store, he took it over when my father died. He was a barber too. My mother died of cancer 20 years after my father. When she died of a cancer I don't think she weighed 80 pounds. In 1959 I did income tax in Albany and lived here. I stayed there until I had a heart attack in '89 and retired.

When we grew up we didn't have the greatest. But I'll tell ya, when I grew up in the 30's it was like a big family, everybody helped everybody. You didn't have to lock the doors.

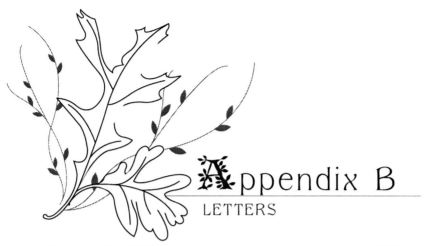

Appendix B

LETTERS

By the early 1960's progress began to encroach upon Oak Hill. A concerned young citizen wrote the following letter.

Oak Hill, N.Y.

April 6, 1964

Dear Rural Road Commissioner,

I'm 13 years old and I live in the nice town of Oak Hill, New York, Greene County. We have many beautiful fields and trees that overlook the Catskill Mountains.

For the past years that I've been able to know what's what, there have been many nice country roads and nice trees that have been cut. Many roads have been remodeled...In making these roads, all trees, regardless of beauty, have been ruthlessly cut down for progress, so I'm told.

I would like to know very sincerely why every little rural road with houses at least a mile apart on these roads that they have to be made wide highways. Some of these roads have not even a half dozen cars going up or down through a day. I feel that the Lord has made us a nice world and that these trees being a waste, I can't understand. I can't help but wonder if the people who plan this realize what is being done and the mess that has been made. For I know it takes years for trees to grow as beautiful as ours.

Could someone from your department give me a reason that I can understand? This would be appreciated.

Yours truly,
Curtis Ellis
Oak Hill, N.Y. 12460
Box 65

Within two weeks he received the following reply.

Dear Curtis:

Thank you for the descriptive letter of April 6 expressing concern over the removal of many trees in order that rural roads may be improved.

You are fortunate in living in the scenic Catskill Mountain area, bountifully supplied by nature. There are millions who are obliged to reside in cities and, when time permits, are anxious to view the fields and streams that afford you so much pleasure. Their method of transportation necessitates the construction of highways. Not to be forgotten are the substantial number of residents of the rural areas who obtain their livelihood by serving the tourists. These, too, are among the many who are seeking better roads.

The Supervisor of your town is Mr. Kenneth R. Hill, Cornwallville, N.Y., who is intimately acquainted with the... improvements now underway. This gentleman is well known to this department and I feel certain that he would be happy to discuss the highway problems that cause you much distress. Furthermore, try to persuade Mr. Hill to invite you to a Town Board meeting. I believe you would find it interesting and a help in your civics course.

Many years ago, the celebrated philosopher, Ralph Waldo Emerson, wrote in one of his famous essays: "He who knows what sweets and virtues are in the ground, the waters, the plants, the heavens, and how to come at these enchantments, is the rich and royal man." I really believe this applies to you.

Sincerely,

J. Burch McMorran

Superintendent of Public Works

The next letter was written near the end of the Civil War by Nathan Augustus to his Oak Hill friend and neighbor James H. Tripp. I have modernized the language.

March 12, 1865

Camp of the 120 Regt N.Y. St Vol.

Camped near Petersburg, Va.

Friend James,

I thought I would write a few lines to you and stating that I am well and hoping these few lines will find you and your folks all well. As it is a long time since I have been in Oak Hill or heard from there and I made up my mind that you hadn't all gone off to war and so I thought I'd write a few lines to you to see if it was so or not, to pass away the lonesome hours in camp.

James, there is nothing new here at present, only the Rebs are deserting and are coming into our lines in large numbers most every night and they say that the rebellion is gone up but that is the old story with them all.

The weather has been very fine here for the past three days and it is thought here that W.G. Grant will open an early spring campaign but, James, I hope it will not be hard for us, as it was last summer. For we suffered awful and had very hard fighting. James, a man to home can't tell nothing about how a poor soldier has to contend with down here for he is exposed to all the bad weather rain or shine.

But I like soldiering very well for we have got used to it, but James, if I am so lucky as to get through with five months more and then I have served Uncle Sam and my country faithfully three years and I have done my duty like a soldier and a gentleman and if I ever live to get out of the army James I shall never be sorry for it, for I have learned something by it.

Our regiment numbers only four hundred men for duty. The health of the regiment is very good and it is commanded by Lieutenant Colonel Lockwood and he is very well liked by all the officers and men and the regiment has done some very hard fighting and it stands today the best regiment in the brigade.

James, I suppose business is dull in Oak Hill at least I hear it. And things have changed some and some have got married. Amos Webb is married, he writes to me so, and Hurk is to Troy to work with him. I saw Edy Hallenbeck the other day, I was over to see him, he was well. We have heard that Billy Hallenbeck has been discharged. I hope he has been for Billy was a good soldier. We had 11 men taken at James City and out of the 11 we have two left, the rest have died in prison in Richmond. Chancey Layman, he died there.

So no more for the present, please write as soon as you can, James.

This is from a friend. Nathan Augustus to a friend James H. Tripp.

Please write all the news and how you all get along, Sudy Jones is well and so is Zan Layman.

Direct 120th Regt. N.Y. State Vol. Third Brigade Third Division Camp K second Washington D.C. brigade first brigade in the first division of the first army

Appendix C
POETRY

Although he will probably be best remembered for his assemblages, Norman Hasselriis took great pride in his poetry. Two examples of his work follow.

hay there, summer

> country road
> wheelin' slow
> sure sign of summer
> no fishin' pole on line
> compact stereo on belt instead
> earphones muffed over head
>
> country roadside
> girl tanned & blonde
> astride blonde horse
> no stereo of course
> two manes loose reins
> plop plop plop plop

idling country stream
high booted fisherman

clambering over rocks
playing line for trout
swatting gnats and flies
that's what summer's about

country hillside
black & white cows
lumps folded in half
dotting green pasture
seriously ruminatin'
idly day dreamin'
dim erotic fantasies
ticklish milking machines

country barn
high in hayloft
boy without bike
girl without horse
no farmer or cows in sight
sneezing seizing
hay
what's goin'on up there

In the Sculpture Garden, Oak Hill

In maple's shade early one morn in late July
I settle back, relaxing in the shaky wicker chair
(bought for one dollar at auction, in need of more repairs)...
eye following the clothesline swooping flights
of a pair of jetstream aviators, the golden finches
who gourmet dine upon the garden's widespread unprinted menu:
seeds of cornflower, peppermint, catkins of the silver birch...

recalling my erratic flights, far less spectacular and sure,
in search of seeds and flowers less tangible
to satisfy vague hungers lingering and whispering
in hollows of question-shaped ear...

and how the other day I once again remembered you, Old Things,
and opened up the 6" stack of high-shelved folders
where you've been lounging, waiting patiently,
never a sigh or peep or musical beep to remind me
of my promises of '78,
yesterday's 7 centuries ago and echoed clearly now.

There were other works to do, other promises to keep,
as well as those writ plainly for you to know
as guardians appointed of the self slowly emergent.
and last year she winked and slyly seduced me, Demeter did,
enslaved me through last Spring & Summer –
our first serious affair (after flirting once before)...
and I was willing weeder, digger, planter, raker, mulcher, picker,

greedy muncher and swallower of her tempting fruits,
chef of her Kitchen Garden and Host
to a few million wee customers
who neglected to make reservations in advance.

Three, four or more gray tons of pebble, stone and rock, I swear,
I dug and raked and barrowed off down path to creek's rough edge...
to clear the central densely weed choked plot,
the ornamental clearing with seven stone-framed beds
not known officially as the Sculpture Garden...
love's labors abundantly repaid in August with bountiful supplies
enough to feast a family of seven.

And in September, to win her favors just once more,
began the monumental work along the creek,
the bridges to the island and the pools between,
and roamed upstream and down with sturdy staff
in search for flood swept vagrant weathered roots along the banks...
to plant an indoor Winter Garden where soon there grew
a whole new family four score and more of poeTrees
and other creatures strange, known sometimes as assemblages.

In the early 1990's Route 81 was reconstructed and widened. A number of healthy, beautiful old trees were needlessly removed. In response I wrote the following poem.

Oak Hill

The rain hears hard
that
there are no trees on Main Street
and down the way "For Sale" signs
are interspersed among the apple blossoms.

Before you and me
squirrels flew from tree to tree
from Maine to Florida without
touching ground.

But look around
the rain hears hard,
there are no trees on Main Street.

Once, the sky was black with geese
and once the land was forever, but no more.
Now forever has come and gone.
Gone.

A future of abject acceptance
of tolerance of fools
of saluting the flag
of obeying the rules

as they chop and sever and kill and destroy
in the name of progress,
like Nature's their toy.

Turn on the faucets
see black water flow.
Turn off your mind
see another's power grow.
Turn around and look and see
all that remains for you and for me.

The rain hears hard.

I wrote the following poem as a result of what I've learned doing research for this book.

Paradox Found

When dense fog was the
only stranger that came and went
then water slid down
the sides of already aged mountains.

Coursing through a soon
to be, an always was, Oak Hill.
And walking out and up onto the banks
are souls of Indians and
ministers and farmers and
factory workers and artists
and home makers and dreamers
and dreams.

They are there but once and
they are there always
like the creek that brought
them and brings them still.
Continuity of
change, finds forever refuge,
finds home, in Oak Hill.

Photo Credits

Author's Collection

Betty Cernik (nee Lounsbury)

Carol A. Cooke

Helen Hulbert

Ralph Hull

Donald Lounsbury

Loretta Lounsbury

Janet Nelson (nee Hull)

Harriet Rasmussen

Terraserver

William Winans

Works Consulted

Arabski, Jessica. "I.U. Tripp & Co: A Treasure Trove of Antiques and History." *Greenville Press* 27 July 2000: 7.

"Artful Economist: Oak Hill's Hasselriis Makes Canny Art." *Mountain Eagle* (Greene County, NY) 9 Nov. 1995: 1.

Atkinson, Brooks. Letter to Carl Ratsch. Private collection. 28 Mar. 1945.

Atkinson, Oriana. *Not Only Ours: A Story of Greene County , N.Y.* Cornwallville, N.Y.: Hope Farm Press, 1985.

Augustus, Nathan. Letter to Eli Peck. Private collection. 28 Sept. 1863.

---. Letter to James H. Tripp. Private collection. 21 Mar. 1865.

Bates, Henry H. Letter to Dr. Abel. N.Y. State Archieves. Albany, N.Y.: 20 Mar. 1863.

Beecher, Raymond. "A Brief History of Oak Hill." *Greene County Historical Journal*, 15.2 Summer (1991): 11-20.

---. *Out to Greenville and Beyond: Historical Sketches of Greene County.* Coxsackie, N.Y.: The Greene County Historical Society Press, 1997.

---, ed. *Greene County: A Bicentennial Overview.* Coxsackie, N.Y.: The Greene County Historical Society Press, 2000.

Bell, Thelma. "Durham Remembered." *Greenville Press* 29 June 2000: N. pag.

Bowers, Douglas E. "Cooking Trends Echo Changing Roles of Women." *Food Review* Jan.–Apr. 2000: 23-29.

Burnett, Alfred. Diary. 8 Feb. 1917 to 8 Apr. 1917. Private collection.

Chadwick, George Halcott, and Jessie Van Vechten Vedder, eds. *The "Old Times" Corner.* Catskill, N.Y.: Recorder, 1932.

"Cobb Permitted to Plead Guilty to Lesser Count." *Recorder* (Catskill, N.Y.) 14 Feb. 1936: 1.

"Cobb Sentenced 20 Years to Life." *Daily Examiner* (Greene County, N.Y.) 18 Feb. 1936: 1.

Cobb, William. Statement to District Attorney, John C. Welch. 9 Sept. 1935.

Cooke, Carol A. Personal interview. July 2006.

Cusator, Elizabeth. *Daily Mail* (Catskill, N.Y.) 28 Sept. 1978: 10.

"Dr. Mahlon Atkinson Testified as to Effects of Alcoholic Beverages." *Daily Examiner* (Greene County, N.Y.) 12 Feb. 1936: 1.

Death Certification. Nathan Augustus. *Town of Durham Records.* Oak Hill, N.Y. Bk 1 P 23. 30 Nov. 1884.

---. Page T. Hoagland. *Town of Durham Records.* Oak Hill, N.Y. Bk 3 P 328. 10 Aug. 1932.

---. Carrie Hodges. *Town of Durham Records.* Oak Hill, N.Y.: Bk 3 P 337. 28 May 1933.

---. Ned Hodges. *Town of Durham Records.* Oak Hill, N.Y. Bk 5

Pg 3. 10 Sept. 1935.

Durham Town Hall Records. Oak Hill, N.Y.: Sept. 1908 to Dec. 2005.

---. Brandow Park renovated. 5 Aug. 1968: 16.

---. Loretta Lounsbury addressed the Town Board. 14 Nov. 1978.

---. Margaret Cooke assumes position on Town Council. 2 Jan. 1986: 176.

---. New Firehouse. Apr.1978.

---. Street Lights in Oak Hill. Sept. 1930: 86.

---. Town Building to be built. 26 Mar. 1971: 81.

Ellis, Curtis. Letter to Rural Road Commissioner. *Town of Durham Records*. Oak Hill, N.Y. Town Records. 11 June 1964: 75.

Elsbree, Hugh. *Twentieth Century Memories of Baseball in Preston Hollow*. Preston Hollow, N.Y.: Privately Printed, 1999.

Elsbree, Willard. Personal interview. July 2006.

Ethan. Personal interview. Sept. 2006.

Eudy, Connie. Personal interview. Aug. 2006.

Federal Census Record. Seventh Census of the United States: 1850. Durham Town. Greene County. Lines 5 – 10. 16 July 1850: 10.

---. Eighth Census of the United States: 1860. Durham Town. Greene County. Lines 38 – 40. 27 June 1860: 53.

---. Ninth Census of the United States: 1870. Durham Town. Greene County. Lines 27-28. 31 Aug. 1870: 153.

---. Fourteenth Census of the United States: 1920. Durham

Town. Supervisor's District 8, Enumeration District 62. N.Y.: 2 Jan. to 14 Feb. 1920. 1A-12B.

---. Fourteenth Census of the United States: 1920. Stanton District. Supervisor's District 5, Enumeration District 104. Halifax, Va.: 2 Mar. 1920. 4A.

---. Fifteenth Census of the United States: 1930. Durham Town. Enumeration District 20-15, Supervisor's District 18. N.Y.: 2 Apr. 1930 - 28 Apr. 1930. 1A-7A.

---. Fifteenth Census of the United States: 1930. Durham Town. Enumeration District 20-16, Supervisor's District 18. N.Y.: 2 Apr. 1930 – 15 Apr. 1930. 1A-5B.

---. Fifteenth Census of the United States: 1930. Roanoke Magisterial District. Enumeration District 42-22, Supervisor's District 11. Halifax, Va. 15 Apr. 1930. 11B.

Fleurent, Vernona Haskins, and Mary Helen Francis Haskins, comps. *Rebels at Rest.* Durham, N.Y.: Durham Center Museum, Inc., 1977.

Ford, Lionel. Personal interview. July 2006.

Frost, Robert. "The Pasture." *Complete Poems of Robert Frost.* New York, N.Y.: Henry Holt and Company, 1959: 1.

"Girl is Held in Bail of $5,000." *Recorder* (Catskill, N.Y.) 20 Sept.1935: 1.

Hamm, Anna. Personal interview. Oct. 2005.

Hard Choices. Dir. Rick King. With Margaret Klenck and Gary McCleery. Karl –Lorimar Home Video, 1984.

Haskins, Vernon. *The Canajoharie – Catskill Railroad 1832 - 1840.* East Durham, N.Y.: Durham Center Museum, Inc., 1967.

---. *Lyman Tremain: Lawyer - Statesman.* East Durham, N.Y.: Durham Center Museum, Inc., 1969.

"Has No Knowledge of Slaying, He Says." *Daily Examiner* (Greene County, N.Y.) 13 Feb. 1936: 1.

Hasselriis, Norman. *Third Avenue Flat: A New Collection of Some Elderly, Long-Neglected Poems.* Oak Hill, N.Y.: The Assemblage, 1997.

---. *Poet in Residence, Oak Hill: A New Collection of Poems.* Oak Hill, N.Y.: The Assemblage, 2001.

---. Personal interview. Feb. 2006.

Hayes, Thad. Telephone interview. Sept. 2006.

Helmer, William F. *Rip Van Winkle Railroads.* Hensonville, N.Y.: Black Dome Press Corp., 1999.

Heidorf, Christian J. *Shoulder Arms! Letters and Recollections of the 22nd New York Volunteers and a Community at War.* Glens Falls, N.Y.: Chapman Historical Museum of the Glens Falls - Queensbury Historical Association, 1998.

History of the Organization of the First Presbyterian Church of Durham Greene County, N.Y. Cornwallville, N.Y.: Hope Farm Press, 1976.

"Hodges Girl Held Under $5,000 Bail." *Daily Examiner* (Greene County, N.Y.) 13 Sept. 1935: 1.

Hodges, Olive. Statement to District Attorney, John C. Welch. 9 Sept. 1935.

Honeyford, Lyle B., M.D. Report of Findings of Autopsy on Body of Ned Hodges, 20 Sept. 1935.

Hulbert, Helen. Personal interview. May - June 2004.

Hull, Joyce. Personal interview. Mar. - Apr. 2004.

Hull, Ralph. Personal interview. Mar. - Apr. 2004.

Ives, Floyd Jr. Personal interview. Dec. 2004.

Ives, Sheldon and Evie Alger. "Oak Hill in 1930: As I Remember It." *Greenville Local* 26 Apr. 1990: 6.

Kellam, Eugene. Personal interview. Jan. 2005.

Kenyon, P.S. Diary. 1 Jan. 1875 to 31 Dec. 1875. Private collection.

Levine, Gary. *Jack "Legs" Diamond: Anatomy of a Gangster.* Fleischmanns, N.Y.: Purple Mountain Press, 1995.

Lounsbury, Donald. Personal interview. Nov. 2005.

Lounsbury, Edward. Diary. 1910. Private collection.

Lounsbury, Loretta. Personal interview. Nov. 2005.

Mabey, Kenneth. Personal interview. July 2006.

Mattice, Burt. Personal interview. Nov. 2005.

McIntosh, Robert P. *The Forests of the Catskill Mountains, New York.* Cornwallville, N.Y.: Hope Farm Press, 1977.

McMorran, J. Burch. Letter to Curtis Ellis. Oak Hill, N.Y. *Town of Durham Records.* 11 June 1964: 75.

"Mid'burgh Drops Three Out of Four." *Middleburgh News* 9 July 1936: 1.

Millen, Patricia E. *Bare Trees: Zadock Pratt, Master Tanner; & The Story of What Happened to the Catskill Mountain Forests.* Hensonville, N.Y.: Black Dome Press Corp., 1995.

"Murder Shocks Oak Hill Folks." *Daily Examiner* (Greene County, N.Y.) 10 Sept. 1935: 8.

"Murdered Man Buried." *Daily Examiner* (Greene County, N.Y.) 11 Sept. 1935: 1.

Nahas, Nick. Personal interview. July 2006.

National Archives and Records Administration. Nathan

Augustus Military and Pension File.

---. Henry Howard Bates Military File.

National Personnel Records Center. Carl O. Ratsch Military Personnel Records.

"Ned Hodges is Killed." *Daily Examiner* (Greene County, N.Y.) 9 Sept. 1935: 1.

Newman, Kopper. "The World According to Norm Hasselriis." *Mountain Eagle* (Greene County, N.Y.) 28 Sept. 2000: B1.

New York State Census Record. 1892. Durham Town. Greene County. 1st Election District 16 Feb. 1892: 1–12.

---. 1905. Durham Town. Greene County. 1st Election District. 1 June 1905: 11-16.

---. 1915. Durham Town. Greene County. 1st Election District. 1st Assembly District. 1 June 1915: 9-14.

---. 1925. Durham Town. Greene County. 1st Election District. 1st Assembly District. 1 June 1925: 1-3.

"Oak Hill." *Middleburgh News* 25 April 1935

"Oak Hill Man Shot to Death." *Recorder* (Catskill, N.Y.) 13 Sept. 1935: 1.

Peterson, Roger Tory. *A Field Guide to the Birds East of the Rockies*. Boston, Mass.: Houghton Mifflin Company, 1980.

"Play with Preston Hollow Sod Busters of Suburban Loop." *Knickerbocker Press* (Albany, N.Y.) 29 May 1932.

"Preston Hollow to Play Colored Champions." *Middleburgh News* 5 Sept. 1935: 1.

"Preston Hollow Victors." *Middleburgh News* 20 Aug. 1936.

Quaker Records. Friends Historical Library of Swarthmore. Minutes of Oak Hill Preparative Meetings, 1812 – 1820.

Rasmussen, Harriet. Personal interview. May - June 2006.

Ratsch, Carl. *Return to the Catskills.* Oak Hill, N.Y.: Big Acorn Press, 1946.

---. *The Land of the Lavender Lizard.* Unpublished. Private collection, 1948.

---. Wartime letters to family and friends. Private collection. Apr. 1942 to Dec. 1945.

"Restaurant Opens in Oak Hill." *Daily Mail* (Catskill, N.Y.) 1991: N. pag.

"Revolver in Oak Hill Murder Case Causes Arrest." *Daily Examiner* (Greene County, N.Y.) 11 Sept. 1935: 1.

Ross, Claire L. and Edward R. Kozacek. *Greene County, New York '76 Bicentennial Overview: Beginnings and Background.* Catskill, N.Y.: Catskill Enterprise, 1976.

Russel, Howard S. *A Long, Deep Furrow: Three Centuries of Farming in New England.* Hanover, N.H.: University Press of New England, 1982.

"Sam Stickler, 37, Dies; Supervisor of Musicals." *New York Times* 1 Sept. 1992: D-17.

"Scenes From Film Shot at Ives' Flats." *Greenville Local* 3 Nov. 1983: 1.

Schumann, Anson. Personal interview. Sept. 2006.

"Services Held for Leo Ford." *Greene County News* 29 June 1967: 4.

"Seventy-seventh Infantry Hits South of Ormoc." *New York Times* 8 Dec.1944: 1.

Siebert, Wilbur H. *The Underground Railroad From Slavery to Freedom: A Comprehensive History.* Mineola, N.Y.: Dover Publications, Inc., 2006.

Slung, Michele. "On the Perpetual Enchantment of Assemblage: Finding Norman Hasselriis." *Albany Center Galleries Brochure* 2 May 2006: 5-6.

Smart, Paul. "Assemblage of a Lifetime." *Ulster Publishing's alm@nac* 18 May 2006: 10.

Smith, Larry. Telephone interview. Feb. 2006.

"Sod Busters to Play Black Sox." *Middleburgh News* 13 Aug. 1936: 1.

Stiefel Laboratories. *Stiefel Yesterday. Stiefel Today & Tomorrow.* Company Publication.

Stickler, Sara. Personal interview. Aug. 2006.

Stickler, Lee. Personal interview. Aug. 2006.

T. Leo Ford. *Daily Mail* (Catskill, N.Y.) 26 June 1967: 10.

Tiano, Charlie. *More Balls Than Strikes: 120 Years of Baseball in New York's Hudson Valley.* Saugerties, N.Y.: Hope Farm Press, 1995.

"Toward Manila." *New York Times* 18 Dec. 1944: 1E.

Town of Durham Salutes Its Past, 1776-1976: A Bicentennial Booklet. Oak Hill, N.Y.: Big Acorn Press, 1976.

Tripp, Wendell. *The Church at the Farmers' Museum: 1791-1964.* Cooperstown, N.Y.: New York State Historical Association, 1964.

Trudeau, Noah Andre. *Gettysburg: A Testing of Courage.* New York, N.Y.: Harper Collins, 2003.

The Twelve Tribes. The Commonwealth of Israel. www.twelvetribes.com/whoweare/.html.

"Two Murder Cases to be Tried in County in '36." *Recorder* (Catskill, NY) 6 Dec. 1935: 1.

United Methodist Church Records. Vedder Library. Coxsackie, N.Y.

---. Private collection.

Van Loan, Walton. *Van Loan's Catskill Mountain Guide with Bird's-Eye View, Maps and Choice Illustrations.* New York, N.Y.: The Aldine Publishing Company, 1879.

Van Santvoord, C. *The One Hundred and Twentieth Regiment New York State Volunteers: A Narrative of Its Service in the War for the Union.* Cornwallville, N.Y.: Hope Farm Press, 1983.

Van Vechten Vedder, J. *History of Greene County Vol. I 1651-1800.* Saugerties, N.Y.: Hope Farm Press, 1991.

"White Man Involved in Murder Trial Here." *Daily Examiner* (Greene County, N.Y.) 11 Feb.1936: 8.

"William Cobb Pleads to Indictment for Murder." *Daily Examiner* (Greene County, N.Y.) 26 Sept. 1935: 1.

Winans, William. Personal interview. Sept. 2006.

Woodruff, Harold C. *Daily Mail* (Catskill, N.Y.) 11 June 1969.

Wright, Porter. "The First 150 Years: A Short History of Medusa." Privately Printed.

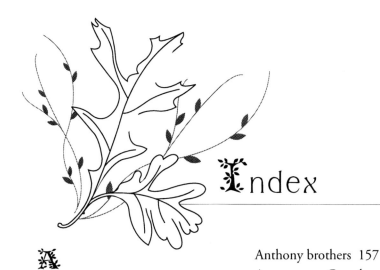

Index

Bates, Wilma 121
Bates Hollow, N.Y. 123
Battle of the Wilderness 8
Beechert, Ed 110
Benton Harbor, Mich. 57
Beverly Hillbillies 66
Bible 60, 78, 152
Birchett, Francis 18
Black Sox 56
Booth, Dorothy 102
Boston, Mass. 151, 152, 153, 154
Bott, Dr. Kenneth 39
Box-Inside a Box Mounted on
    Thread Spool 75
Brand, Mr. 60
Brandow, Leroy 19, 53, 57, 58, 133
Brazil 78, 152
Brick House 16, 84, 94, 141
British 2
British Army 2
Broadway 65, 66
Brockett, Elenor 102
Bronze Star 45
Brooklyn, N.Y. 56, 132, 133
Brooklyn Royal Giants 56, 132,
    160, 165
Brother Duck and Sister Duck 74
Bryant, Al 145
Bullivant, Alfred 135
Bullivant, Elvira 27, 28, 122, 135,
    148
Bulson, S.L. 39
Burnett, Alfred 13, 14, 15, 16, 17,
    19, 20, 21, 22, 30, 53, 59, 61,
    83, 84, 85, 107, 133, 135,
    137, 141, 142, 143, 145, 155,
    164, 165

Burnett, Calvin 15, 85, 93, 136,
    141, 142, 164
Burnett, Carrie 15, 85, 142, 143
Burnett, Elizabeth (nee Griffin) 15,
    30, 84, 85, 135, 141, 142,
    143
Burnett, Shirley 102, 103, 135, 136
Burns, Tom 111

Cahill Road 135
Cairo, N.Y. 2, 141, 142, 143, 144,
    145, 150
California 66
Campo Road, Ashland, N.Y. 117
Canada 2, 78, 152, 161
Canajoharie, N.Y. 3, 4
Canajoharie and Catskill Railroad 4,
    128, 167
Carlin, Jim 85
Catskill, N.Y. 1, 3, 37, 39, 54, 129,
    144
Catskill Baseball Team 54
Catskill Creek 1, 2, 3, 11, 17, 52,
    81, 118, 120, 127, 139, 164,
    167
Catskill Mountains 13, 42, 45, 46,
    52, 85, 91, 171, 172
Catskill Valley Historical Society 49
Central School 136
Chattanooga, TN. 77
Cheritree, Olive 71, 85
Cheritree's Inn 64, 95, 120, 168
Cheritree Foundry 3, 129, 167
China 48
Christians 77, 78, 138
Christian Hill 14, 84, 138, 142

Goff, William 19
Gourd Man with Straw Hat 75
Grant, Ulysses S. 8, 174
Grease 66
Great Depression 20, 29, 30, 34,
    130, 157
Greene County 35, 67, 79, 126,
    134, 171, 193
Greene County Historical Society
    67, 79
Greenville, N.Y. 18, 132, 139, 141,
    145, 148, 150, 165
Greenwood, N.Y. 133
Guam 44, 45

Hale, Horatio 161
Hall, Annie 143
Hall, Byron 15, 16, 84, 141, 143,
    164
Hall, Hattie 15, 84, 144
Hall, Lou 143
Hallenbeck, Billy 174
Hallenbeck, Edy 174
Halloween 60, 129
Hall and Burnett's 15, 16, 31, 64,
    81, 84, 92, 94, 122, 133, 136,
    137, 141, 145, 158, 162, 169
Hamm, Anna 28, 135
Hard Choices (film) 71
Haskins, Dow 109
Hasselriis, Malthe 72
Hasselriis, Norman 72, 73, 74, 75,
    76, 84, 111, 177
Hasselriis, Ruth 72
Hatcher's Run, Petersburg, VA. 5
Hawaii 44

Hayes, Hugh 144
Hayes, Margaret 144
Hayes, Thad 67
hay there, summer 177
Hello Dolly 65
High Rock 4, 52, 64, 100, 127,
    128, 167
Hill, Kenneth R. 172
Hilzinger, Helen 59, 60
Hilzinger, Raymond 19
Hoagland, Page P.T. 17, 21, 22, 71,
    85
Hodges, Carrie 34, 85
Hodges, Carrie B. 34
Hodges, Dabner 34, 38, 40, 160
Hodges, Dorothy 34
Hodges, Lee 160
Hodges, Lena 34
Hodges, Mollie 34
Hodges, Ned 22, 34, 35, 36, 37, 38,
    39, 40
Hodges, Olive Bell Olie 20, 34, 35,
    36, 37, 38, 39, 40, 83
Hodges, Robert 34, 39
Hodges family 22, 34, 35, 40
Hodges house 37, 83
Honeyford, Dr. Lyle B. 39
Horning 24, 119
House of David 57, 155
Hudson River 1, 3, 19
Hulbert, Alfred 53, 54, 85
Hulbert, Glen 146
Hulbert, Helen (nee Kellam) 40,
    42, 84, 102, 108, 111, 120,
    125, 156, 161, 166
Hulbert, Llewellyn Bud 40, 102

About the Author

Michael Hayes has a Master's Degree in American History and has taught U.S. History as an Adjunct Professor at the State University of New York. He has contributed to the Long Island Historical Journal and has had a number of his original poems published. Currently Mike is a teacher in the Social Studies Department in East Meadow High School. He serves as President of the Oak Hill Preservation Association. Mike divides his time between his homes on Long Island and in Oak Hill.

Printed in the United States
79986LV00002B/445-531